REIKI
FOR BEGINNERS

THE ESSENTIAL GUIDE TO HEALING YOUR MIND, BODY, AND SOUL

LISA VITALE

TABLE OF CONTENTS

INTRODUCTION

Reiki is a system of energy healing. Its modern forms originated in early 20th century Japan. Reiki shares some traits of other Eastern healing medical practices in which physical health is viewed as directly dependent on the distribution of energy throughout the physical body. However, unlike many forms of alternative medicinal practices, Reiki has found acceptance within the mainstream of Western medicine and science. Although not regulated by any official governmental agency, Reiki practitioners have formed many independent professional associations that have resulted in fairly uniform training and education methods.

Reiki takes a holistic view of healthcare. Not only have patients suffering from a wide range of illnesses found relief using Reiki, but so also have many otherwise healthy practitioners seeking effective methods of self-growth and development. Reiki is compatible with the yogic traditions of the chakras. In addition, Reiki has the capacity to act as an effective supplement to conventional Western medicine.

The scientific advances of contemporary Western cultures have helped determine the course of history for centuries. Yet, as these technological advances continue to increase exponentially, the benefits of alternative treatments like Reiki have become increasingly apparent. Through the religious traditions of Judeo-Christianity, the West has acknowledged the validity of claims that potentially fatal physical illnesses may be cured spiritually vis-à-vis that teachings and practices of Jesus Christ. Those traditions are continued today mostly through the practice of the Anointing of the Sick, a Holy Sacrament practiced by priests of the Catholic Church. Similarly, through the practice of exorcism, the Catholic Church in the West has acknowledged the validity of claims of demonic possession.

The contemporary era is dominated by empirical science, technology, and modern medical procedures that usually require the intervention of medication and surgery to be considered valid. Belief in claims of faith healing and demonic possession have become almost completely absent from mainstream society and exist almost entirely in marginalized subcultures. Japan's spiritual and intellectual culture are radically different from Western cultural practices. Japanese culture has always acknowledged the greatness of the teachings of Jesus Christ. However, their spiritual practices differ fundamentally from Western religions in that they are not founded upon the belief in the absolute contrast between good and evil that Judeo-Christian teaching requires its followers to accept. As a result, their approach to spiritual healing and other forms of alternative medicine also differ. To understand the effectiveness of Reiki, readers should first acknowledge this cultural gulf. Though the claims made by practitioners of Reiki are based upon cultural beliefs that the West has made an effort to eradicate, large numbers of people around the world have attested to the ability of the simple methods used in Reiki healing to restore balance and help them attain lasting health and well-being.

CHAPTER - 1
HISTORY OF REIKI

Anyone interested in undertaking a study of Reiki or using it as a healing or spiritual practice in daily life should begin by considering the varied history of this practice. Many people regard Reiki at best as a harmless but useless pseudoscience, and at worst as a controversial and potentially dangerous superstition. Reiki flourished rapidly after it was initially established and soon gained worldwide recognition. Its founders went on to receive great praise and reward from the highest echelons of Japan's scientific, business, and military societies. However, the rapid changes brought about by industrialization and the resulting conflicts in World Wars I and II imposed many challenges to traditional societies around the world. As a result, many of the established institutions that had existed prior to the 20th century were forced to transform themselves in order to survive; many of them have been lost to us.

Reikiwasestablishedduringthetumultuousness dawn of the early 20th century. Although Reiki teaching and practice in the 21st century have undergone much change and revision, most of its original history has been preserved intact. This chapter provides an overview of that history.

What is Reiki?

Reiki is a Japanese word that means "universal life force energy." The chakras are understood to be spinning wheels or balls of energy that distribute life force energy throughout the subtle energy body that surrounds each of our physical bodies. This life force energy distributed by chakras is known in Sanskrit as "prana." Reiki draws upon the same concept of a universal life force energy. Traditional Chinese medicine also refers to this type of energy, using the term "chi."

Although the practice of Reiki draws upon this knowledge of an invisible life force energy, the practice of Reiki differs from other practices that incorporate the use of prana or chi. Reiki in practice is used specifically to help people heal from illnesses. Furthermore, although all professional practitioners of Reiki healing must be able to treat themselves, Reiki healing differs from practices like yoga in that it is possible for a patient to be treated using Reiki healing without first becoming proficient in Reiki themselves.

As a form of alternative medicine, Reiki is most commonly used to help people heal from both physical and psychological illnesses and diseases. A typical Reiki session involves the patient lying flat in a deep state of relaxation while the Reiki practitioner passes his or hers hands over the patient's body. The Reiki practitioner—or Reiki Master as they are officially known—will have been previously attuned to Reiki energy and capable of creating a shift in the energy of the patient, ultimately helping to restore balance to the flow of energy throughout their body and thereby helping them to achieve a state of health and well-being.

All practitioners of Reiki healing must undergo training by a Reiki Master. This training consists not only of how to conduct Reiki healing sessions, but also includes attunement of the new practitioner to enable him or her to conduct the Reiki energy through his or her hands and pass it on to the body of the patient.

For many reasons, Reiki healing practices remain unregulated throughout the world. Due to this lack of formalized regulations, Reiki healing practices may differ in their methods and techniques. However, all of them adhere to the same basic core principles that will be outlined later in this book.

Especially in the West, most forms of alternative medicine are regarded as having less credibility and effectiveness than practices based on hard science and empirical research. In addition, businesses that operate outside the official framework of governmental regulation do not receive the same degree of official acceptance and recognition as licensed and regulated professions. As a result, there is some disagreement about whether Reiki is an effective treatment method.

Regardless, many people throughout the world who have undergone Reiki healing treatment or training as a Reiki healer have stated that this practice has made a tremendous difference in their ability to attain a state of health, vitality, and well-being. Despite the lack of regulation or governmental oversight, many hospitals and medical facilities have endorsed the use of Reiki as a supplemental treatment, particularly for patients undergoing surgery. Many organizations—including the National Institutes of Health (NIH)—are making an effort to conduct qualified research that can help to establish Reiki as an accepted practice.

When and Where Was Reiki Developed?

Prior to the era in which the modern practices of Reiki healing were developed, Japan had been a very closed, insular, and feudal society. Beginning in 1641, people of European descent had been expelled from Japan, Japanese citizens were not permitted to leave, Christianity was declared illegal, and all Japanese citizens were required to officially register at temples of Shino Buddhism. The use of ancient systems like the channeling of Reiki healing energy was practiced during this time. In the 1850s, Japan began to reopen itself to the outside world. In 1873, the United States forced Japan to lift its ban on Christianity and open its borders. From that point, Japan underwent an extremely rapid period of development and industrialization and new forms of thought, industry, and philosophy quickly turned Japan's closed and feudal society into a churning and turbulent mix of innovation and change.

As Japan was emerging from its long self-imposed exile, many people in Japan were motivated by a desire to resist the rapid pace of change by reintroducing traditional Japanese cultural practices. There is some disagreement about the original formation of Reiki healing, due mostly to the fact that Reiki healing practices can be traced to ancient Japanese cultural traditions. However, the modern practice of Reiki healing as it is known throughout the world today, can be traced to the work of Dr. Mikao Usui.

Dr. Usui was born in 1865 Miyma-cho, Japan. His efforts in the field of Reiki began in earnest in 1922. However, prior to his discoveries, there were several schools of Reiki healing already in use throughout Japan. In 1914, the Japanese therapist Matiji Kawakami had developed a form of healing practice he called Reiki ryoho, the Japanese term for Reiki healing. Dr. Kawakami published his work in 1919. In addition, at least three other schools of energy healing were also in use at that time, including reikan tonetsu ryoho, created by Reikaku Ishinuki; senshinryu Reiki ryoho, created by Kogetsu Matsubara; and seido reishosjutsu, created by Resisen Oyama.

Thus, Reiki healing practice can ultimately trace

its lineage to ancient Japanese feudal society. However, the modern practices of Reiki as we know them today result from a rediscovery of traditional culture that was underway droning Japan's period of modernization in the late 19th century. The worldwide phenomenon of modern Reiki healing today can be traced to March 1922, with several important developments in its evolution occurring in both Japan and the United States throughout the remainder of the 20th century.

Who Developed Reiki?

The modern practice of Reiki is generally attributed to the work of Dr. Mikao Usui. Many contemporary Reiki Masters often refer to Dr. Usui using the Japanese term of reverence, Usui Sensei. Although Dr. Usui founded established what would become the model for the modern practice of Reiki in 1922, his history of involvement in this field dates back much further.

According to the inscription on the memorial stone that marks his grave, Mikao Usui was born in Taniai Village in the Gifu Prefecture of the Yamagata District of Japan in 1865. Dr. Usui is the descendant of Tsunetane Chiba, a military commander of the Heian Period of 1180 to

1230. During his childhood, despite his family's wealth, he experienced many of the difficulties typical to people of the time and region, but he showed a lot of promise as a student. While completing his academic career at Japanese Tendai Buddhist Monastery, he received training in Samurai swordsmanship and Kiko, a Japanese form of the traditional Chinese medical practice of Chi Kung. Dr. Usui was influenced by a wide variety of developments in medicine, energy movement, and religions.

His inquiries led him to further educational pursuits in China, Europe, and America, but his studies eventually led him back to Buddhism, and upon his return to Japan, he became a Tendai Buddhist monk and took up residence in a monastery near Mount Kurama.

As a teacher, he encountered a student who had asked him how Jesus Christ had facilitated all the miraculous tales of healing that appeared in the Bible. Dr. Usui was stuck for an answer, but this question provided inspiration and motivation for much of the work he accomplished in the latter half of his life. Much of his work at that time was focused on finding a way to heal himself and his patients using his hands. His research led him to rediscover the ancient tradition of Reiki energy healing.

While pursuing these objectives, he became a member of the Rei Jyutu Ka, a Japanese society of metaphysical researchers focused on developing psychic abilities. Working as a civil servant, an employee at many companies, and as a journalist, he explored ways of putting his knowledge to use by helping to rehabilitate prisoners. As the Secretary to Shinpei Goto, Head of the Department of Health and Welfare and later the mayor of Tokyo, he made many connections that helped him to become successful in business.

Ultimately, however, his focus on developing enlightened healing practices became the driving force of his life. Frustrated with his inability to make the kind of progress he believed was possible, he sought the guidance of a Zen teacher who taught him Zazen meditation. After three years of practice, his teacher recommended a radical course of action intended to intensify the experience of metaphysical enlightenment. During this personal quest to seek heightened spiritual truth, he spent 22 days fasting and meditating at the top of a mountain, and toward the end of this period, in a state of weakness and exhaustion, he attained the state of enlightenment he had been seeking. As he was coming down the mountain to relate his experience, he stumbled and injured his toe. When he stopped to examine the damage, he touched the injury with his hands and watched as the wound was miraculously healed. Thus, he unexpectedly found he had acquired the ability to channel through his hands the healing power of Reiki energy.

This discovery prompted him to establish a healing society he called Usui Reiki Ryoho Gakkai (Usui Reiki Healing Method Society) in April 1922, along with an additional healing clinic in Tokyo. From 1922 until his death in 1926, he traveled throughout Japan teaching students and healing the sick and wounded. He established two official methods of Reiki healing—the Shin-Shin Kai-Zen Usui Reiki Ryo-Ho (The Usui Reiki Treatment Method for Improvement of Body and Mind) and the simplified form known as Usui Reiki Ryoho (Usui Reiki Healing Method).

Before he died, he was widely acclaimed throughout Japan, personally trained 2,000 students and approved them as both practitioners and teachers of Reiki healing and received the Kun San To award from the Japanese government for doing honorable work to help others.

After his death, his students erected a memorial at his gravesite and his teachings were passed on from generation to generation, ultimately spreading around the world and leading to the modern Reiki healing practices we know today.

Why Was Reiki Developed?

Despite Dr. Usui's extensive background in medicine and a lifelong search for a method of healing through touching and energy manipulation, Reiki as we know it today was not the result of a linear progression or a deliberate effort to formalize and establish Reiki as an officially recognized treatment method.

Dr. Usui's extensive work in the areas of academia and research, medicine, business, religion, and combat resulted from his drive to discover the purpose of life. Seen in this light, all of his work as a student, and subsequently as a monk, a professional, as a teacher, and as a civil servant were driven by his unquenchable thirst to find meaning in the world around him and to impart that knowledge to others in an effort to make the world a richer and more worthwhile place.

As a monk, he occupied a unique position that gave him the advantage of access to spiritual knowledge and guidance. He was much freer to pursue his goals by engaging in deep meditation in an effort to find the answers to his many questions by seeking enlightenment. Through these studies, he became aware of the special state of consciousness that had been identified as the key to understanding life's purpose, as well as finding the means of achieving this purpose. This state of consciousness was known in Japanese as An-shin Ritus-mei. He learned that anyone who attained this state of consciousness will not only be able to understand and achieve his purpose but will also remain permanently in this state without making any additional effort.

However, although Dr. Usui understood this concept form an intellectual perspective, he had been frustrated in his efforts to actually attain this state of enlightenment through his practice. The Zen teacher under whom he studied prior to his discovery of the Reiki healing method advised him that his only hope of finally attaining this state of consciousness was to undertake an extreme form of meditation in which the subject had to be willing to accept death as the requirement.

When Dr. Usui began his 22 days of fasting on Mount Kurama, north of Kyoto, he expected that he would only attain this state of consciousness as he passed into the next world. Thus, during this time, far from looking for the method of healing he had been so passionately seeking, Dr. Usui was trying to attain a spiritual state that he believed would result in his death.

The practice Dr. Usui undertook on Mount Kurama involved standing under a small waterfall in such a way that the water striking directly on the top of the head activates the crown chakra to initiate the state of An-shin Ritus-mei. As Dr. Usui pursued fasting, meditation, and stimulation of the crown chakra, he began losing strength. Eventually, he was struck in his mind by a powerful light entering through the top of his head that jolted him physically like an electrical charge, and he fell unconscious.

When he emerged from his trance, the fatigue and hunger had vanished, and he was filled with energy, vitality, and an extreme sense of pleasure. His normal state of consciousness had been replaced by An-shin Ritus-mei. This excitement led him to injure himself as he ran down the mountain to share the news with his teacher. When the painful injury he sustained in his foot immediately subsided with the touch of his hands, he realized he had received the gift of Reiki healing, which was how it was revealed to him that the purpose of his life was to be a healer and that the means of doing so was to teach as many students as possible and to set up healing clinics wherever the need was greatest.

Dr. Usui's subsequent activities in establishing his healing and teaching clinics allowed him to treat thousands of people in the wake of the great tsunami and earthquake of 1923 in Tokyo. This urgency also prompted him to increase the pace at which he trained new students. All of the efforts Dr. Usui made in the next several years before his death—including the development of hand gestures, symbols, and attunement ceremonies—he made in an effort to carry out what he believed was his life's purpose. For this reason, the core principles of Reiki healing transcend merely the goals of healing acute physical and psychological ailments and challenges patients to reconsider their entire approach to daily living.

Origins of Reiki Around the World

The lineage of the modern practice of Reiki healing has been traced back definitively to Dr. Mikao Usui. Dr. Usui made tremendous progress in the few final years of his life, from discovering the healing power of Reiki to establishing teaching and healing clinics. From that point forward, the development of Reiki as an established practice in Japan and the subsequent spread of Reiki healing to countries around the world is a somewhat more complicated story.

Immediately following his discovery in 1922, Dr. Usui saw in the Great Kanto earthquake and fire of 1923 an opportunity to apply himself to what he now believed was the purpose of his life— to use his powers as a healer to help as many people as possible. His initial efforts resulted in the development of practitioner methods and techniques that included Gassho, Byosen scanning, Reiji-ho, Gyoshi ho, and Seishin-to-itsu. He also formalized a method of attuning new students so that they, too, could draw upon the healing energy of Reiki and transmit it to their patients. This attunement method was known as Reiju kai, and those who completed this training were expected not only to continue their work as healers, but also as teachers of Reiki, so that new healers would be continually added to the growing society of Reiki healing. Dr. Usui also developed many of the symbols still used in Reiki today.

In its original form, Reiki training included repeated attunement sessions to ensure that students' ability to draw upon and transmit Reiki energy was continually enhanced. Dr. Usui understood that Reiki was an infinitely renewable source of energy, and that there was no limit to the amount or degree of healing energy to which any student should be limited by.

By 1925, demand for the service of Dr. Usui and all of the students he had trained overwhelmed the abilities of his initial clinic, so he opened a second clinic in 1925. After receiving a high honor from the Japanese government, he passed away a year later, and the continuation of his practice was left in the hands of those he had trained.

The first to take the lead in continuing the practices of Dr. Usui was Chujiro Hayashi, a former naval officer who had previously opened his own Reiki clinic. After Dr. Usui's death, Hayashi began his own school and clinic—the

Hayashi Reiki Kenkyukai. Based on his extensive recordkeeping of the patients he treated using the techniques established by Dr. Usui, Hayashi began formalized these practices further. He established various hand positions and created a manual so that training would be more uniform and effective. He made some additional refinements to the methods established by Dr. Usui, such as requiring patients to lie down for treatment rather than sit in a chair, as had been done previously.

Hayashi traveled to Hawaii in 1937 prior to Japan's attack on the United States, and on his return, the Japanese government pressured him to provide information about the locations of potential targets. Hayahsi refused, was declared a traitor, and was forced to commit seppuku, or ritual suicide, according to Japanese tradition. Hayashi's wife took over the clinic, but when she retired several years later, no one was available to assume the responsibilities of running the clinic, which eventually closed.

During the time after Hayashi's passing, Reiki practice became scattered once again, and it wasn't until 1999 that one of Hayashi's Master students—Chiyoko Yamaguchi—emerged as one of many who had maintained the teachings originally introduced by Dr. Usui. Yamaguchi began teaching Reiki to younger generations, so that by the time she died in 2003, enough of the original teachings had been preserved to enable a renaissance.

Meanwhile, Hawayo Takata was born in Hawaii in 1900. At the age of 34, she was widowed and left to raise two children. The toil took its toll on her health, and eventually she traveled to Japan to seek treatment. Here, she was introduced to Reiki healing, and though she was initially suspicious of the claims of the practitioners who had treated her, her recovery convinced her of the value of Reiki healing. She sought training from Chujiro Hayashi and became certified, and it was Takata whom Hayashi was visiting in Hawaii prior to his death upon his return to Japan.

Because Takata was much more familiar with Western culture than any of her fellow practitioners in Japan, she was instrumental in establishing a simplified, Westernized method of teaching and passing on the Reiki healing methods initially established by Dr. Usui. She established several clinics in Hawaii and taught her simplified methods to many students. Before she died in 1949, she had trained 22 Reiki

Masters, and healed and worked with many others. Takata's work provided the means by which Reiki was eventually introduced to every country in the world, and without her efforts, all the practices established in 1922 may likely have fallen back into obscurity.

After World War II, the conditions of unconditional surrender imposed on Japan were accompanied by a requirement that all people who offered any kind of healing must acquire licensing and answer to a regulatory authority. Although some clinics did cooperate, the general view was that Reiki practice would be preserved best by going underground. This view is still prevalent and the reason why most clinics today are still unlicensed and unregulated.

CHAPTER - 2
FUNDAMENTALS OF REIKI

In the practice of tantric yoga, the chakras are recognized as energy centers—literally, spinning wheels of energy—distributed around the region of our physical body throughout what is known as the subtle body or energy body. The chakras distribute life energy that the tantric traditions call "prana." There is more information about Reiki's relationship to the chakras in Chapter 6, but for now, to understand the fundamentals of Reiki, it is important to establish that Reiki, like "prana," is a term that means "universal life energy."

Chapter 1 discussed how the established practice of Reiki healing did not follow from any deliberate, conscious effort to discover new methods of spiritual or faith healing. Instead, it was the serendipitous result of a scholar and monk engaged on an entirely different quest. Moreover, due to the complications of modernization following the initial discovery of Reiki and its practitioners' desires to protect the practice from Westernized control, Reiki healing practices in Japan are unregulated as a rule. Furthermore, the atmosphere of empirical skepticism along with the culture of regulation in the West have resulted in a chaotic network of decentralized, scattered, and unregulated Reiki healing practices disconnected from any centralized authority. Regardless, enough literature exists to formulate a unified theory of fundamentals common across all forms of Reiki practice. This chapter provides those details.

What Is the Purpose of Reiki?

Before stating definitively what the purpose of Reiki is, it is important to remember that there is a difference between the term "Reiki" and the term "Reiki healing." Remember that Reiki is a Japanese word that means "universal life force energy." Thus, Reiki is energy, and at the most literal level, it does not have any purpose except the uses to which we put it.

Throughout this book—as in most contemporary practice—the terms "Reiki" and "Reiki healing" are used interchangeably. This will be the case unless it is necessary to make a distinction between the energy itself and the use of that energy to impart healing.

Yogis often refer to the subtle energy body, the invisible field of energy that surrounds everyone's physical body, and through which the chakras distribute prana energy. Reiki healers call this energy field an "aura."

Normally, we are sustained both physically and psychologically by the nourishing and vitalizing energy of the aura. Whenever the aura is disrupted by negative thoughts or destructive actions, it becomes infected and loses its ability to sustain our state of continual health, energy, and optimism. Reiki is a particular type of energy that can heal these infections and disruptions in the aura, allowing us to return once again to a state of happiness, well-being, and vitality.

As a result, it may seem easy to conclude from this understanding that the purpose of Reiki is to cure illnesses. However, this definition of Reiki's purpose oversimplifies the nature of Reiki and the history of its development as an established practice of physical and psychological healing.

To be clear, Reiki healing has developed along two distinct paths. The first path of development followed from the work Dr. Mikao Usui. Dr. Usui discovered Reiki energy and its capacity to enable advanced, deep healing quite by accident. Although well-acquainted with medical science, Dr. Usui's spent much of his life seeking answers to philosophical, religious, spiritual, and metaphysical questions, rather than looking for cures to any specific diseases.

Prior to his discovery of Reiki, Dr. Usui was immersed in a deeply committed pursuit of meditation in an effort to understand the purpose and meaning of life in general, and of the purpose of his life as an individual. Thus, he discovered Reiki as a result of pursuing enlightenment to gain insight into profound questions concerning humanity's destiny. For Dr. Usui, the discovery of Reiki was an unexpected but welcome reward to his quest. He did not hesitate to develop to the greatest capacity he could manage a means through which the practice of Reiki could lead to healing the illnesses and diseases of as many people as possible.

Yet, from his perspective, Reiki's usefulness in medicine was really a by-product of his own search for meaning and purpose. For Dr. Usui, it was wonderful to discover Reiki's power to heal physical ailments, but what seemed more

important was that Reiki's capacity to heal

disruptions in the aura could allow an individual to gain insight into one's own existential and spiritual states. From this perspective, attaining physical health was only a step in the larger process of acquiring health and vitality in these higher states of consciousness.

After Dr. Usui's revolutionary discovery of the healing capacity of Reiki and his newfound ability to channel this energy, he immediately received the support and assistance of Dr. Chujiro Hayashi. Dr. Hayashi's experience in the Japanese Navy was mostly dedicated to serving the first aid needs of wounded soldiers.

Dr. Hayashi knew of Dr. Usui's reputation as a monk and teacher, and certainly respected his accomplishments in those areas. However, Dr. Hayashi's motivations were entirely different from those of Dr. Usui. Dr. Hayashi was not so much interested in determining the purpose of his life, or whether there was any larger significance to humanity's existence, as he was in learning about the practical aspects of setting up medical treatment clinics and how training in Reiki healing could be formally established.

This picture was complicated further by the fact that Dr. Usui's mystical experience inspired him to see the purpose of his life as healing the sick and the poor. As a result, his response to Dr. Hayashi's requests were enthusiastic, and together they made tremendous progress early on.

The picture gets even more complicated after that. Hawayo Takata's visit to Japan from Hawaii, and Dr. Hayashi's death after his return from a visit to Takata in Hawaii around the time of World War II had two major results: the direct lineage of Reiki teaching in Japan was severed; and the seeds of knowledge of Reiki healing were planted in the West. The tumultuous and turbulent changes that have echoed around the world since the dawn of the twentieth century have added considerable complexity and opacity to the development of Reiki.

Thus, the purpose of Reiki may differ from one patient and one teacher to the next. For some, Reiki healing may be nothing more than a simple alternative medical treatment used in conjunction with conventional medicine to help them recover from an acute onset of a physical illness or disease. For others, Reiki healing provides a means to establish an entirely new way of life through ongoing treatment and daily practices of self-care that lead to self-actualization and personal happiness and fulfillment.

The Five Principles of Reiki

Dr. Usui formulated the Five Reiki Principles. In his original formulation of Reiki instruction, learning the Five Reiki Principles was taught very early on. Today, the same five principles are taught during the Level One course. They still represent the fundamental core of practices that allow Reiki healing energy to provide a lasting foundation for lifelong happiness and success.

Dr. Usui's view of health and medicine was very holistic. Remember that at the time he discovered the healing power or Reiki, he was seeking enlightenment and a meaning and purpose to life. Many people—especially in the modern world—are often confronted by what seems to be the unsolvable problem of the futility of life. Often, this discovery of futility can be oppressive and claustrophobic and make us feel like no matter what we do, our lives are a waste of time. Often, such feelings can lead us into destructive and harmful behavior. Though our motivations may often be genuine frustration and sadness over our seemingly incurable condition of hopelessness and despair, self-absorption in feelings of pity, remorse, anger, resentment, and self-indulgence—no matter how justified—generally only make things worse. Too often, such a condition can lead to a downward spiral, and soon the feeling of annoyance or sadness that disrupted our day may have erupted into a serious case of mental or even physical distress and illness, sometimes leading to disease and death.

Dr. Usui did not view illness and disease as solely a physical problem requiring only physical interventions. Similarly, he did not view health as merely a state in which the physical body is free of any diagnosable disease. Instead, a healthy physical body was the means by which we could attain our life's purpose. As one cannot bang a nail into a block of wood without a hammer, so one cannot achieve one's mission in life without a healthy physical presence.

In the West, the domain of medicine is limited exclusively to the physical. The foundation of Reiki healing is that lasting physical health can only be achieved in those who have attained spiritual health. This is the motivation for incorporating healing of the aura into the healing of the physical body—because a healthy aura can maintain the health of the physical body without the constant intervention of pills and surgery.

So, the Five Reiki Principles express the underlying philosophy by which all practitioners of Reiki healing should live to ensure that they will continue to channel the healing power of Reiki. The Five Reiki Principles are:

1. Just for today, do not be angry.

2. Just for today, do not worry.

3. Just for today, be grateful.

4. Just for today, work with diligence.

5. Just for today, be kind to people.

These principles seem easy enough to understand and to apply. In fact, they are fairly straightforward, and most people, whether or not they engage in the practice of Reiki healing, can derive great benefit from living according to these principles.

However, these principles were originally formulated in Japanese. Once translated into English, they lose some of the nuance and complexity inherent in the original Japanese; in addition, native speakers of English familiar with the vocabulary and structure of English may overlook the considerable complexity of these deceptively simple expressions. For this reason, this section will examine each of these principles individually.

1.   Just for today...

Each of the principles begin with this mantra. But many people may misinterpret why this introduction is included and repeated throughout the five principles. The mantra "just for today," is not intended to convey the idea that we should not maintain these principles every day, all the time. For example, "Just for today, do not be angry," does not mean that it is okay not to be angry for one day, then return to a state of anger once the day of peace is concluded. Nor does it mean that you should keep the principles only on the days you want to channel the healing power of Reiki. Instead, each principle is preceded by this mantra precisely because Dr. Usui recognized the difficulty of living life according to principle. Telling anyone that for the rest of their life, they must never be angry and never worry and exist in a perpetual and eternal state of diligent gratefulness and kindness would likely have the opposite effect intended. By asking us to adhere to each principle "just for one day," channeling the healing power of Reiki becomes possible. Tomorrow is another day, and you can cross that bridge when you come to it.

2.   Do not be angry.

This principle may seem difficult or even impossible. Especially in the modern world, the constant whir of violent and frenzied activity of competition, status-seeking, meanness, and pressure to keep up eventually causes even the most level-headed among us to occasionally erupt or break down in an angry outburst. Anger is a natural human emotion and can even be a healthy response when we have been lied to, wronged, disrespected or abused. But feeling anger as a rational response to an isolated incident is entirely different from occupying a mindset in which everything we do is motivated by anger. Anger is a dangerous emotion that can consume all of your life energy, drain your spirit, and cause us to act in ways that may cause grave emotional and even physical illnesses.

3.   Do not worry.

As with anger, so too with worry. Most people spend a lot of their time lost in worry. The modern world imposes ideals of false competition and fosters the illusion that unless we attain a predefined amount of monetary wealth, social status, and physical beauty, we will have failed in life. In such environments, it is not humanly possible to avoid some degree of worry. Yet, worry is precisely the emotion that will prevent you from attaining these goals. No one can do it all in one day, so it is better to let go of worry. Once your mind is composed and calm and free of worry, you will be free to apply yourself diligently and completely to the pursuits that matter.

4.   Be grateful.

Being grateful can seem like an exercise in silliness. The modern world has recognized that we are all living in conditions in which the distribution of wealth is not only unequal, but also unjust, much of it a result of deliberate acts of corruption. So, asking someone to be grateful in the face of such injustice can seem like asking too much. However, remember that what we want when we think we want money and wealth and power, is not really money or wealth or power. It is what those qualities bring: the ability to feel happy, and grateful, and free from worry. So score a victory against the forces of oppression by finding something to feel grateful for today—they can't take that away from you.

5.   Work with diligence.

Diligence is a word that many people rarely use, except in the context of the legal requirements governing the issuance of corporate financial statements. Due diligence in banking is entirely different from ordinary diligence. And diligence itself has begun to acquire an archaic connotation of naivete and obsolescence. Yet, this principle is not trying to express either. In the sense of this principle, to be diligent in your work means that you are wholly and completely dedicated and given over to it. However, you make a living, whatever your profession or vocation or calling, you should not regard it as a chore, but as your chosen path in life. When you achieve this goal, your work will no longer feel like a burden, and the diligence with which you pursue success will flow naturally and easily and allow you to inhabit permanently the state of freedom you once sought to purchase with money and diversions.

6.   Be kind to people.

The professional world has been called the "soul-killing world of business." Often, we are told that success in business will only be earned through shrewdness and hard-hearted commitment to making the tough decisions. There is undoubtedly some truth to this sentiment—no one has ever become a billionaire by handing out money and hugs. However, it is equally simplistic to believe that simple being mean is the key to financial success. Remember that the purpose of business is to provide goods and services; and that, for the most part, people want to buy goods and services so they can be happier and enjoy their life in the world. There is a goal beyond hitting the annual sales record, and if you focus on that goal, your sales numbers will fall into place. Remember also that all creatures great and small deserve the same kindness you would show to your best friend, so be nice to trees and animals, too.

These are the Five Reiki Principles. For just one day, you can do it.

The Three Pillars of Reiki

The five principles of Reiki embody the kind of respectful, harmonious, and serene state of mind and body representative of a person who is free of suffering, illness, and disease. The Reiki healer and teacher hopes to help the patient and student to achieve such a state. The Reiki healer and teacher must live according to these principles if he or she hopes to be able to access and use the three pillars of Reiki.

The three pillars of Reiki are like the three legs of a stool. Unless all three legs of the stool are firmly bolted to the seat and even in length, the stool will be unbalanced, unsteady, and will not be able to serve its intended purpose well. Although the three pillars of Reiki are related to the three levels of Reiki, they are different in that all three pillars are a fundamental and necessary aspect of every treatment session.

The Japanese words for each of the three levels of Reiki are:

- Gassho

- Reiji-Ho

- Chiryo

Gassho

Gassho is a Japanese word originally derived from Middle Chinese. The Japanese word is spelled,合掌, and combines two words-合, or gatsu, meaning "unite"—and 掌, or shó, meaning "hands." Thus, gassho is a Japanese word for a gesture in which the hands are held together as in prayer. You may be familiar with the term, "namaste," which is often used in yoga and may be regarded as a synonym for gassho.

The purpose of gassho, the first pillar of Reiki healing, is to allow the healer or teacher to enter a state of receptiveness to so that he or she may begin channeling the Reiki healing energy.

Especially in the West, students are taught to enter gassho by placing their hands together as if in prayer in preparation for a period of meditation. Students are often taught that gassho can be completed by focusing on where the middle fingertips meet. However, while this is certainly valuable and necessary guidance, entering a state of gassho is somewhat more complex.

Spiritual cleansing

There are two primary reasons a Reiki healer must engage in gassho. The first reason is to enable purification and spiritual cleansing. Remember that the Reiki healer will be channeling Reiki in an effort to help his or her healing partner recover from some type of illness or disease. If the healer has not attained a state of gassho in which his or her mind is free of distraction or impure intention, he or she may not be able to effectively channel the healing energy.

Each healer may develop a particular ritual through which gassho enables the spiritual cleansing and attainment of intellectual clarity and focus necessary to perform Reiki healing. Regardless, once you have secured and prepared your area, gassho should begin by sitting comfortably, placing your hands in prayer position, then quietly focusing on your breathing and the place where your middle fingertips meet. Breathe deep, steady, relaxed breaths through your nose, as you feel the air come in through the top of your body and exit as you exhale.

As you focus on your breathing, you will feel the tension, preoccupation, worry, anger, frustration, fear, or whatever else that has plagued you throughout the day slowly vanish and drift away. There is no time limit or specific set of movements to make here, but stay focused in this relaxed state of centered meditation until you feel you are free of your attachments, calm, and at peace. This is the only state in which you will be able to transmit Reiki to your student or patient.

Setting a healing intention and provide a foundation for healing

Another reason for gassho is to set a healing

intention as you begin a session. When your student or patient has joined you after you have prepared using gassho meditation, you will begin by standing at their head, once again entering gassho, focusing on the healing goal you have agreed upon for the session, and asking for guidance to use the session to attain only the highest of goals. This state is also where you will first begin to draw in the Reiki as you begin treatment.

In addition, throughout the treatment session, you may find that you become distracted. Sometimes the world outside may intrude. Sometimes, your patient may be unusually distressed. Sometimes, the trauma may be so severe that you experience shock or disruption. Whenever this happens, you can regain control of the session by once again returning to gassho.

Reiji-Ho

The Japanese term Reiji-ho, or 霊示法, is a combination of the Japanese words 霊, or rei, meaning spiritual pointing; 示 ,or ji, meaning revealing or showing; and 法, or ho, meaning way, rule, law, or method. Thus, Reiji-ho is the pillar in which the Reiki healer asks of the Reiki to be revealed to him or her that he or she may connect with its healing power.

Once a healer has entered gassho and set the healing intention, he or she should ask for guidance using reiji-ho. One cannot enter a state of reiji-ho unless one first enters a state of gassho. In a state of gassho, the healer must begin to listen deeply and intently to your mind, your body, and all of your senses. You must also listen intently to hear and perceive the needs and demands of your patient or student. Only with your fullest and most intent focus, and only with the highest of intentions will the healer be able to connect his or capacity to channel Reiki.

In this state, your mind and body become the vessel through which Reiki is channeled and through which you transmit its healing power to your patient or student. No two sessions and no two healers are exactly alike in the way in which Reiki is detected, accessed, channeled, and transmitted. Whether your guidance comes in the form of an intuitive sense, or whether you are guided by external clues on the body or aura of your patient, channeling and working with Reiki effectively takes intense concentration and effort.

Once you learn how to detect and direct the presence of Reiki, you must learn to allow your intuition and the Reiki to direct you to the places that need healing and to transmit the energy effectively.

Chiryo

Chiryo is the third pillar of Reiki. The Japanese term Chiryo, or 治療, combines two words--治, or rule, and 療, or treatment. Chiryo is generally translated as medical treatment; thus, the chiryo pillar is the Reiki treatment itself.

Chiryo incorporates the Japanese word for rule because effective Reiki treatment must be administered according to the rules of practiced originally established by Dr. Usui, and later by Drs. Hayashi and Tanaka, and now the many, many teachers and practitioners of Reiki around the world.

Chiryo requires the use of pre-established hand positions in places around the patient's body. A Reiki healer will know where the main treatment points are located. Many of them are uniform, but it is also necessary for the healer to become practiced and proficient in learning and inventing new methods, techniques, and locations through which Reiki can be transmitted to foster healing and recovery.

The Five Elements of the Reiki Healing System

The practice of Reiki healing has undergone many changes and transformations since its original inception as a modern practice at the beginning of the 20th century. Reiki healing practice's origins are actually very ancient. Dr. Usui's discovery in the 1920s was based on his earlier scholarly and professional research into many of the traditional practices of ancient Japanese culture. Furthermore, Dr. Usui himself was influenced by many traditions, including the esoteric Buddhist practice known as Mikkyô, the ancient Japanese religious practice of Shugendô, the classical teachings of the Samurai traditions, martial arts training, and medicine. Dr. Usui himself was also motivated largely be his search for meaning and purpose in life, so at the beginning of the 20th century, using Reiki to promote healing was initially a secondary concern.

When the responsibility for managing the administration and teaching of Reiki healing passed from Dr. Usui to Dr. Chujiro and then to Dr. Takata, changes in the methods of Reiki healing were inevitable. Now in the 21st century, the capacity of Reiki to restore physical health and spiritual balance and well-being has gained global acceptance.

Yet, much has changed since Dr. Usui's original discovery in 1922. Not only in Japan, but everywhere, people have turned away from traditional forms of teaching and learning. Many traditional cultures have been extinguished by or absorbed into the larger globalized corporate business model, which does not value many of the forms of knowledge in which Reiki healing is based. Ironically, the values and belief systems supported by this modern, globalized corporate structure lead precisely to the types of imbalances and disruptions that traditional spiritual traditions like Reiki seek to address.

As a result of this process of evolution in the development of Reiki, there is considerable variance in the way in which the five elements of Reiki are taught. Though some schools teach that these five elements are literally the elements that compose the entirety of the practice of Reiki healing—from the basic spiritual concepts, to meditative practices, to symbols and mantras, to hand positions, to attunement. Other schools have developed their own proprietary teaching models that incorporate "Five Elements" into the brand

name. However, despite all the changes, the

fundamental concept of the five Reiki elements has remained a constant and provides a direct link to the traditional beliefs upon which Reiki healing is based.

Traditionally, the five elements theory is based in combines elements of traditional Chinese medicine with the theory of yin and yang. The yin and yang forces are seen as opposite but complementary forces that ultimately produce natural phenomena, with nature correspondingly organized into five separate categories of elements: wood, fire, metal, earth, and water. According to this belief system, nature conforms to two cycles—the Creator Cycle and the Destroyer Cycle. The Creator Cycle is responsible for the elemental interactions of the world. During this cycle, water generates wood; wood generates fire; fire generates metal; metal generates water; and so on. During the Destroyer Cycle, the forces of yin and yang interact and exert control over the elements such that water controls fire; fire controls metal; metal controls wood; wood controls earth; earth controls water; and so on.

Thus, using Reiki energy requires healers to understand the universe as a composite of these elemental interactions, and that each of these elements has significance with regard to the human spiritual condition. Following are descriptions of how each element functions in relation to spiritual balance:

Wood

The wood element is associated with the promise of new life, as in the renewal of life in the spring when trees blossom and once again support the growth that extend the possibility of life to so many others. The wood element is associated with the liver and gallbladder, as well with the eyes and tendons. Blockages or impairments in this area may reveal themselves as migraine headaches, dry, brittle, nail, or pain in the midsection beneath the ribs.

A person's wood element may be out of balance in either direction. An overactive association with a positive influence in this area can lead to an overly extraverted personality with too little energy and attention reserved to ensure the success of one's individual goals. When there is too little influence of this element, the may person may display a disproportionate show of anger, or listlessness, despair, and a complete lack of motivation in pursuing personal goals and interests.

The wood element is associated with springtime, the color green, and flavors that are acidic in nature.

Fire

The fire element is associated with the power and force of life in its fullest bloom and at the height of its vitality. Fire represents that power of direct action, willful intention, strength, vitality, and protection; as well as to drives of lust, destruction, and anger. The fire element is associated with the energy represented by the solar plexus chakra, and so influences our ability to succeed through transformative change and action in the world. The fire element is also associated with the heart and with whole body healing.

The fire element is associated with the capacity to experience mutual joy and respect. When a person has too little influence from the fire element is out of balance, they may become stubborn, greedy, jealous, and develop significant problems with resentment and anger. An overactive fire element can lead to violence, egotism, and domineering behavior. In addition, impairments in this area can result in digestive problems.

The fire element is associated with summertime, the color red, and flavors that are bitter in nature.

Metal

The metal element is associated with the beginning natural decline of power and life. Whereas fire represents that capacity to effect change through direct, forceful action, metal represents a more mature view, with the wisdom gained from experience to know what may be necessary to retain advantages gained through direct action. The metal element is associated with the heart and throat chakras, representing the importance of expressing the need for empathy and understanding. The metal element is associated with the lungs and with healthy circulation and respiration.

The metal element is associated with the capacity to feel sadness and to appreciate that value of justice, bravery, and altruism. When the metal element is underactive, the patient may become overly judgmental; when it is overactive, the patient may experience intense melancholy. Impairments may also include a noticeable lack of energy associated with decreased respiratory function.

The metal element is associated with autumn,

the color white, and flavors that are spicy or sour in nature.

Earth

The earth element is associated with stability, strength, and grounding. The earth element represents the capacity to establish a stable, safe, and balanced environment in which to pursue one's objectives comfortably and confidently. The earth element is most closely associated with the root chakra and the importance of ensuring the basic necessities of life are met. The earth element is associated with the spleen; impairments can result in headaches and fever as a result of the inability of stuck energy that cannot pass completely from the crown chakra to the root chakra.

The earth element is associated with the sense of touch and the capacity to feel compassion and develop healthy self-esteem. Patients with an underactive earth element may experience intense worry or disproportionate concern for their own well-being; patients with an overactive earth element may become overly materialistic, greedy, lazy, and narrow-minded.

The earth element is associated with the end of summer, the color yellow, and flavors that are sweet in nature.

Water

The water element is associated with more altruistic feelings and our capacity to appreciate and value humanity as a whole. We are composed mostly of water, so a balanced water element is important both literally and metaphysically. The water element is associated with emotional balance and stability; it is also associated with the kidney.

When the water element is overactive, the patient may become overly emotional and unable to focus; when it is underactive, the patient's emotional function may become so severely impaired that they overcome with fear and anxiety. A balanced water element allows for the easy expression and maintenance of gratitude, happiness, and serenity.

The water element is associated with winter, the colors blue and black, and flavors that are salty in nature.

CHAPTER - 3

THE LEVELS OF REIKI

Many people seek the benefits of the healing practice of Reiki simply as patients suffering from a variety of physical, psychological, emotional, or spiritual ailments. Such patients may only have learned of Reiki after first being diagnosed with their illness. Many patients may feel "stuck" in their lives or dissatisfied with the results of treatment for their medical doctors. By seeking out a practitioner of Reiki, they may hope to find more complete relief from their condition.

Although Reiki healing is not regulated by any governmental agency medical board, or psychological or psychiatric society, the international community of Reiki practitioners continues to follow the basic methods outlined by the founder of Reiki healing practice. Since its founding, the various schools of Reiki healing have developed several variations and methods of both practice and teaching, but all of them conform to a uniform structure. Certification as a Reiki practitioner is awarded in 3 levels—First Degree, Second Degree, and Third Degree, or the Reiki Master level. To be considered qualified to practice Reiki, the practitioner must have attained at least a First Degree certification from a qualified teacher. This chapter provides specific details about what is involved at each level of training.

First Degree Reiki

First Degree Reiki training is open to anyone who wishes to learn to use Reiki energy healing. There are no prerequisites. The Japanese word for First Degree is Shoden. Basically, First Degree Reiki training includes the study of the official history and tradition of Reiki, an introduction to the use of Reiki for self-treatment as well as for treating others, and an initial attunement that enables the student to begin accessing the powerful force of Reiki energy.

One of the important distinctions of First Degree Reiki training is that it is open to all students and prospective teachers. The next two sections discuss how prerequisites for enrolling in subsequent training, but no such requirements exist at this level.

A second important characteristic of First Degree Reiki training is its focus on the physical applications of Reiki. As previous chapters have discussed, Reiki can help to heal not only physical ailments, but also mental, emotional, psychological, and spiritual disease and illness. However, when students are attuned to Reiki at the First Degree level, the energy they are able to access functions almost exclusively at the physical level. Students who receive attunement in First Degree training will be expected to perform Reiki healing mostly on themselves but will also receive instruction for healing others by transmitting to them the energy that flows through their hands.

Each student will have a unique experience at this level, but typically attunement results in feelings of heat or coolness, or sensations such as tingling or buzzing that occurs in the hands and fingers. Some students have reported feeling an immediate shift in their perceptions with the sense of Reiki flowing through them occurring immediately at the time of attunement. Others have reported a short delay, with sensations beginning a few hours after the intitule attunement. Still others have reported delays of up to a month or more before they notice any change. For this reason, there is usually a required waiting period between First Degree Reiki and Send Degree Reiki training sessions.

The main focus in First Degree Reiki is to help the student learn how to use Reiki on himself or herself. During attunement, the teacher will spend time opening the channels that flow from the crown chakra and opens the student the increased capacity for healing at this level. As a result, there is an expectation that the student will be working toward resolving any issues that may be blocking the passage of energy through the chakras, as well as any other problems or concerns that brought them into Reiki training to begin with.

Once the student is connected to the Universal Energy during the initial attunement, he or she remains connected for the rest of his or her life. The amount and degree of healing energy each student may be able to access after the initial attunement may vary widely from one student to the next, but as the student becomes increasingly proficient and comfortable using the healing energy, the intensity and constancy of this energy tends to grow and then stabilize.

First Degree training represents an abrupt shift in the student's priorities and way of living.

In addition, First Degree training includes initial attunement. Because these significant developments require some time to seek their own level, many teachers will require that students practice self-Reiki, continue focusing on opening their energy channels, and ensure they are committed to the healing practice before continuing to the next level.

It is also important to note that early in its development, First Degree Reiki training was comprised of four discrete levels: Loku-Tou, Go-Tou, Yon-Tou and San-Tou. When Dr. Takata introduced a Westernized model of Reiki to her audience, she combined these four levels into one level, but required that First Degree students undergo four separate attunements. These evolutionary developments in the way in which knowledge of Reiki healing has been communicated around the world may account for any differences you encounter when you pursue Reiki training at this level.

Second Degree Reiki

Second Degree Reiki training is characterized by the initiation of students to the treatment of others. Specifically, Second Degree Reiki training is training at the Practitioner level; successful completion of his level entitles students to begin charging patients for providing healing treatment.

To be accepted into a Second Degree Reiki training class, all applicants must first have successfully completed a First Degree Reiki training course. Some schools and teachers will offer both First Degree and Second Degree Reiki training in one weekend module or other type of multi-day single session. However, most teachers will require a period of anywhere from 21 days to 3 months to have passed after completion of First Degree Reiki training to ensure the student has had time to adjust to the initial attunement and to have had plenty of practice with self-treatment.

The other reason for the required delay between First Degree and Second Degree training is that newly attuned students must be given the opportunity for their newly opened energy channels to establish themselves. Much of Second Degree training involves additional attunements designed to open these channels even further, with a particular focus on the opening of the heart chakra. Typically, Second Degree training involves one additional attunement, though many teachers may provide several additional attunements during these sessions.

The attunements provided during Second Degree training increase the intensity of power and the amount of energy students will be able to access. The central channel will now be more fully opened, and Reiki will begin to flow more fully and steadily into the students' chakra systems.

Students at this level will also receive formal training in the use of hand positions, gassho meditation, Reiji-ho, and Chiryo, as well specific techniques such as Byosen scanning, in which the practitioner uses the Reiki flowing through his or hands to detect areas of stress in the patient's body and aura.

Finally, Second Degree Reiki training, students receive three "Reiki Symbols." The symbols each represent a different component of how Reiki can be channeled and used to heal others. The three symbols received at this level are:

Power Symbol

The Japanese term for the Power Symbol is Cho Ku Ray, which has been translated as both, " I have the key," and "God and man coming together." The purpose of the power symbol is to allow the practitioner to increase the amount of Reiki to which he or she has access. By using the power symbol, the practitioner can open or close the connection to Reiki, thereby enabling the cleansing and purification of physical and energy spaces. To use the power symbol, the practitioner must draw the symbol over himself or herself and/or his or her patient and recite the words "Cho Ku Ray" three times, silently.

Mental Symbol

The Japanese term for the Mental Symbol is Sei Hei Ki, which has been translated as both, "The Key to the Universe," and, "God and man coming together." The mental symbol allows the practitioner to enter a different level of Reiki energy. Whereas the initial attunement allows the student to access mostly the physical healing aspects of Reiki, the mental symbol can allow him or her to transform this healing energy to address ailments associated with mental and emotional anguish and suffering. Once again, the practitioner must draw the symbol over himself or herself and his or her patient while reciting, "Sei Hei Ki." The Reiki energy will be attuned to address issues such as healing emotional or psychological trauma; emotional imbalances that result in unhealthy amounts of anger, sadness, or anxiety; helping patients remove blockages impairing their emotional function; and stopping habitual habits like smoking.

Distance Symbol

The Japanese term for this symbol is "Hon Sha Ze Sho Nen," which has been translated as, "The God in Me Greets the God In You to Promote Enlightenment and Peace." Students who have been attuned to this symbol in Second Degree training are able as practitioners to send healing over distances of time and space. When using the distance symbol, the patient does not need to be physically present; instead, the practitioner can draw the symbol and recite the phrase, "Hon Sha Ze Sho Nen," before transmitting the healing power of Reiki to an individual patient at a distant location. This symbol also works across time, allowing the practitioner to heal past traumas and wounds, or prepare participants in a future event to help ensure their success.

Third Degree Reiki/Reiki Master

The Japanese term for Third Degree Reiki training is Shinpiden. Third Degree training is sometimes combined with Master Level training. This section discusses both levels separately. First, the goal of Third Degree Reiki training is to enable students eventually to become Reiki Masters.

During Third Degree training, students receive additional attunements to improve their ability to channel Reiki healing energy and to increase the power and intensity of that healing energy. In addition, Third Degree training requires students to focus more on spiritual healing components. Third Degree students will be better equipped to work with patients who complain about spiritual ailments. For this reason, the training at this level is also known as Inner Master training because it focuses students on developing an awareness that each of us is master of his or her own destiny. Third Degree students are better equipped to treat patients suffering from existential and spiritual crises by helping them find internal healing and direction. This use of Reiki healing is closer to the purposes and motivations of the founder, Dr. Mikao Usui.

Because of the difference in application and focus from Second to Third Degree, students are generally encouraged to wait a considerable amount of time between Second Degree and

Third Degree training. After Second degree training, students should spend time gaining experience as practitioners and gain some degree of comfort and expertise in applying their skills as healers. The intense shift toward more spiritual and deeply personal healing benefits from time spent working at the Second Level.

Master Symbol

In addition, Third Degree students also receive the Master Symbol. The Japanese term for the Master Symbol is Dai Ki Myo, which has been translated as both, "Great Enlightenment," and, "Great Shining Light." The Master Symbol should be used by Third Degree students to establish a connection to the divine, and to facilitate healing at all levels.

Third Degree students who have been attuned to the Master Symbol are encouraged to invoke this symbol prior to all of their healing sessions. Invocation of this symbol, as with those others, requires drawing the symbol over oneself while reciting, "Dai Ki Myo." Invocation results in enhanced and more powerful healing across all forms of Reiki practice. Some examples of how Third Degree students use the Master Symbol include:

- Enhancing the connection between the practitioner and Reiki to facilitate deep healing at the level of the soul.

- Healing and opening of the chakras and the aura

- Healing illness and disease from its original source at the level of the spiritual self.

- Drawing out and releasing negative energy from both the physical body and spiritual energy body.

- Developing and strengthening personal and spiritual growth and development, self-awareness, and intuition.

- Increasing the ability of the healer to attain a higher state of enlightenment and become more psychic.

- Strengthening of the immune system and increasing energy flow throughout the body.

- Enhancing the existing healing properties of herbs, medicines, or homeopathic remedies.

- Used in combination with other Reiki symbols, the Master Symbol can help increase the effectiveness of those symbols. For example, invoking the Master Symbol before using the Distance Symbol can speed the transfer of healing energy over distance.

- Healers attuned to this symbol can purify and bring a higher dimension of light to all their healing practices.

- Finally, the Master Symbol is used by Reiki Masters to open channels during Reiki attunement and to attune new students who want to become Reiki practitioners.

Reiki Master

Finally, the Reiki Master level, which is sometimes combined with Third Degree training, is reserved for students who wish to become teachers to pass on the knowledge of Reiki to new practitioners. At the Master Level, students receive a Master attunement and training in how to attune others. This instruction in the attunement of others is what separates Master Level training form Third Degree training.

In addition, at the Master Level, there is generally an expectation of serious commitment from all students, and Master Level training explores more deeply and widely the varied applications of Reiki healing. For example, Tibetan Master Level training includes instruction in the use of four additional symbols—the Tibetan Master Symbols. Reiki Masters are uniquely equipped not only to provide a wide array of highly specialized healing practices to treat many types of illnesses and diseases, but also to train new students and to conduct their own journeys of self-discovery with renewed insight.

CHAPTER - 4
THE REIKI
HEALING PROCESS

Although Reiki has not been universally accepted, many hospitals and medical facilities have endorsed the use of Reiki as a supplemental treatment, particularly for patients undergoing surgery. Many organizations—including the National Institutes of Health (NIH)—are making an effort to conduct qualified research that can help to establish Reiki as an accepted practice. However, Reiki is currently unregulated and has many critics in the scientific and medical communities. As a result, it is not possible to provide a definitive overview of all that is involved in a Reiki treatment session, nor is it possible to provide a complete list of illnesses for which Reiki has been approved for treatment.

However, despite these irregularities, the fact that Reiki healing follows a central, unified core of governing principles makes it possible to provide an overview of what you should expect to encounter in the Reiki healing process. Whether you are a patient seeking treatment or you are interested in establishing yourself as a Reiki healer, this chapter provides information about the nature of Reiki healing, the generally accepted methods established by the society of Reiki practitioners, and the basic requirements of Reiki practice.

Mind, Body, and Spirit Wholeness

The medical community has recognized that the body's biological functioning is somewhat like a machine in which all of the parts must be in working order and depend upon another to ensure the proper functioning of the whole. The machinery of the human body enables a huge variety of complex functions, such as breathing, digestion, circulation, and the development of antibodies to fight diseases. Each of us is truly a wonder of natural creation.

Yet, we are not merely machines. We do not simply exist to eat, digest, sleep, breath, and fight off disease. These functions allow us to serve the higher purposes of our lives. Each of us is animated with our own personalities, viewpoints, likes, beliefs, and passions, and the biological machinery of our bodies allows us to carry out whatever these more spiritual impulses may drive us toward.

This understanding of a life energy that flows within and around each of us, giving each of us our particular spirit, enthusiasm, and optimism is one way to understand why Reiki practitioners believe Reiki healing should be a fundamental part of your self-care.

Especially in the modern world, each of us is confronted each day by a seemingly endless barrage of challenges, stress-causing situations, frustrations, annoyances, obstructions, inconveniences, and other unfortunate experiences and encounters. The natural restorative power of our bodies' biological machinery is often enough to allow us to recover from these daily attacks, so that we can continue to be productive, happy, and successful.

However, it is not uncommon for the residual effects of stress-inducing encounters to accumulate and take their toll. Any machine, no matter how well-regulated and engineered, will require maintenance if it is expected to continue operating in top condition. When we are weighed down by too many demands or expectations, or burdened with too much disappointment or disruption, our body's ability to restore our naturally optimistic outlook can weaken. Soon, we may begin to adopt pessimistic or negative thoughts or beliefs about ourselves. Though this damage occurs on the psychological and emotional level, it affects the overall ability of the chakras to distribute healthy energy effectively and continually throughout the aura and the physical body. Although viruses and germs can certainly be one cause of disease; and physical injuries another; the emotional and psychological baggage caused by overexposure to stress and worry is at least as potentially deadly.

Most medical treatment works by identifying an illness after it develops, diagnosing it, then treating it with medicine or some other type of physical intervention. This type of treatment is usually effective, but it rarely treats the underlying causes of illness in the patient. For example, a patient with high blood pressure may be prescribed pills and a recommendation for a healthier regimen of diet and exercise, but the treatment usually stops at the end of the doctor's visit. In many cases, the pills may help reduce the symptoms of high blood pressure, but such patients often do not receive any holistic care or ongoing treatment to address the problems that may have caused their high blood pressure to begin with.

Reiki begins the treatment of illnesses by addressing the health of the patient's entire mind-body well-being as a whole. Reiki healing addresses this challenge by channeling Reiki—Universal Energy—throughout your body and aura to restore a natural, balanced, and healthy flow of energy.

Chakra healing treatments such as yoga, meditation, dietary changes, affirmations, and crystal therapy, can help open the flow of energy through the chakras. Reiki takes this treatment a step further. Professional Reiki practitioners are trained to channel the healing Reiki energy itself through their hands and direct it to the disrupted areas of the patient's aura in which interrupted energy flow has resulted in some type of dysfunction. The underlying causes of stress and stress-related illnesses—whether physical, emotional, psychological, or spiritual—can often be traced to an interruption in the flow of energy.

Reiki provides an external source of natural treatment to address the causes of diseases and illnesses. The aim of conventional medicine is to provide an immediate cure for serious physical ailments. Reiki works differently by addressing the causes that may lead to these illnesses in the first place.

Many major hospitals and medical facilities have acknowledged that even patients suffering from potentially deadly illnesses like cancer have shown better responses to recovery when cancer treatment is accompanied by Reiki treatment. Reiki allows patients to boost their body's healing mechanisms, which once again begin to function effectively.

In addition, the stress-reducing benefits of Reiki treatment can help reduce blood pressure, heart rate, and the production of stress-related hormones. This altered state of physiological functioning can enable a shift from a high-adrenaline state of "fight or flight" to a more relaxed state, in which the body's machinery can focus on the production of hormones and chemicals that aid in the process of healing and recovery. By purposely avoiding reliance on medication to initiate this shift, Reiki acts as a means of natural intervention to restore the balance to body, mind, and soul.

Spiritual Awakening and Energy Management

As the historical development of Reiki

attests, there are two main focuses of Reiki practitioners. Most people—especially in the West—have recognized that despite its reputation as a non-scientific alternative medical treatment, Reiki can assist in the recovery and healing process by enabling the body's ability to maintain its capacity for self-healing. This medical application is probably the predominant attraction to Reiki for practitioners and patients.

However, it would be a mistake to assume that Reiki has no usefulness outside its capacity to serve as a supplemental treatment to conventional medicine. The truth is that Reiki was discovered as part of a larger quest for spiritual growth. The capacity to enable growth in this area remains the most important aspect of this healing practice.

The state of relaxation helpful in the recovery of illnesses, and for which Reiki is often used in medical settings, can often be accomplished with the use of medication. But medication fails to provide any lasting foundation for ongoing self-care and cannot help patients outside of the limited effect of artificially lowering blood pressure and stress-related conditions.

Though it can be used to optimize the results

of medical intervention, Reiki itself is not a medical treatment. Reiki is a discipline whereby practitioners, students, and patients alike are made aware of their full capacity as human beings to access the life force energy that exists in that naturally occurring universe.

For most of this, these concepts exist exclusively as esoteric philosophies from an era that has long since receded into history. We have been conditioned to accept many of the stories of the supernatural as they exist in religious teaching or in pop culture artifacts like film and comic books. But generally, our culture has placed them beyond reach.

Reiki first restores our ability to understand that all of the forces are still at play in the world today no less then they were thousands of years ago. Though the world is certainly far more polluted and fuller of obstructions today, the presence of these obstacles does not diminish the power or quantity of Reiki that is available for us.

Once the patient or student has attained a sense of stability, calm, and well-being—especially with regard to his or her immediate physical and psychological health, their path to growth and fulfillment has really only begun.

Consider that a career criminal may convince himself that he is making progress as the seriousness of his crimes increases over time; such people are able to convince themselves that the longer prison sentences they serve as a result of their violations prove their growing success. Ordinary people have a similar problem. As we work longer hours to achieve higher states of productivity to earn the accolades of bosses and colleagues, we often take bigger risks with our emotional and physical health, spend less and less time pursuing what really matters to us, all while convincing ourselves that our increasing unhappiness is proof of our progress on the established path of guaranteed success. During these times, we may have encounters with alternative treatments like Reiki, but most of us are back at our usual routines once the discomfort has passed.

The real value of Reiki begins after we establish a stable state of physical, emotional, psychological, and spiritual health. It is only in this state of enlightened well-being that we can most clearly see the shortcomings of the systems we are often raised to believe are the exclusive means to success and happiness.

Reiki is a total system of self-care that can help you learn to live by placing your spiritual well-being and spiritual aspirations first. It takes considerable time and effort and time it takes to care for the health of the chakras and the entire energy system that nourishes our physical bodies with sustaining life force. Most of us use this time to put in long hours at work, which usually leads us back to a state of spiritual sickness and poverty.

Breaking this cycle is difficult and challenging, but not impossible. Many Reiki practitioners and all Reiki Masters have made a commitment to living according to the practices that allow them to channel Reiki's healing forces. As a result, their paths in life may often differ radically from the average nine-to-five office worker. Many Reiki practitioners are able to incorporate their professional Reiki practice into their more ordinary, daily routine. Others have completely given their time and energy exclusively to the pursuit of this practice of spiritual healing and cleansing.

Working with a certified Reiki Master, you will come closer to understanding that Reiki can provide a foundation for a healthy, disciplined, and rigorous life that leads not only to physical vitality and health, but also to the personal and spiritual growth you were meant to pursue on your human journey.

How to Treat Others

There are some professional organizations such as the International Association of Reiki Professionals (IARP) that provide a framework for uniformity and consistency among treatment methods. However, for the most part, Reiki is an unregulated professional practice, so it is difficult to provide any absolute rules about how a professional practitioner should provide Reiki healing in his or her practice.

Despite the lack of a legal framework, there are some essential components that should be part of any training session. If you are a patient seeking treatment, the first thing to remember is that anyone who has had training can administer Reiki. Such individuals may be professional Reiki practitioners, healthcare providers with training in Reiki, or even a friend or family member who has not provided treatment outside a familiar network of associates. In addition, any setting can be used to provide Reiki healing treatments. Usually, there will be an officially designated area that is quiet, secluded, private, and safe, but such spaces can be set up fairly quickly and easily. Many hospital and healthcare facilities have specific areas and rooms reserved specifically for Reiki treatment. The facilities of many private practices may be similar to what you encounter with massage therapists; in fact, many massage therapists themselves may also be trained in Reiki healing. Other professionals who may also provide Reiki healing include acupuncturists, reflexologists, herbalists, and professional homeopathic medicine dispensers. You can check the bulletin board of local yoga studios or ask at your local hospital if you need additional guidance.

If it is your first time seeking Reiki healing, take the time to find a practitioner you believe you can trust. Ask them about their experience and make sure they can describe the process clearly and accurately. Some practitioners—particularly those with a background in healthcare—may use an intake form that asks some general questions about your health and medical history and whether you are currently suffering from any injuries or other acute trauma.

Practitioners should be able to tell prospective clients specifically what type of training they have received, including the specific level and

training center; how long the classes were and

what they covered; how much time they have spent between levels; whether they have any clinical experience; and whether they use Reiki themselves as a system of self-care. In addition, many Reiki practitioners who belong to a professional association can show they have agreed to comply with a Code of Ethics or carry some type of practitioner insurance.

During a typical session of Reiki, the patient will remain fully clothed. Usually, the patient lies comfortably on his or her back, though sometimes the patient may also be asked to simply sit in an upright position in a chair. The practitioner will use light, non-invasive touching techniques to distribute Reiki energy to the patient's head and upper parts of the front and back torso. Reiki treatment should not involve any inappropriate touching or pressure. Sometimes, the practitioner may also apply additional hand placements on the limbs, especially if there is an injury in a specific area. If the patient has suffered some type of wound or burn, the practitioner will likely offer treatment by keeping the hands just above contact level with the body.

Reactions to Reiki treatment vary widely from one patient to the next. One of the most common reactions is that people will fall into a deep state of relaxation and emerge feeling refreshed and energized. Patients suffering from migraine headaches may often notice that their headache has disappeared. Other patients may notice only a very subtle shift in energy or may not notice any dramatic improvement until after the session has ended.

Typically, a practitioner's hands will generate heat as a result of conducting and distributing Reiki, so many patients may notice a warm and tingling sensation during treatment. Others have described an experience similar to hypnosis, in which they feel as if they are floating or just slightly disembodied, in a state of consciousness between sleep and wakefulness. Frequently, sessions are fairly uneventful, though most patients report a feeling of reduced anxiety and stress. Many patients may also detect physiological adjustments, such as improved digestion, easier and more confident movement and poise, or deeper and better sleep.

How to Treat the Self

Most Reiki professionals use Reiki for self-treatment. At its initial founding, Reiki was less a means of providing supplemental care in the healthcare environment than it was the result of a path of spiritual development. Reiki Masters, of course, are committed to a life founded on the Five Reiki Principles, and all First Degree students must begin professional practice through self-care sessions.

Of course, not all Reiki patients will ultimately become practitioners or even students. Regardless, many hospitals and healthcare facilities support the use of Reiki, particularly as a form of supplementary self-care for post-surgical cancer patients. In these contexts, patients often receive self-care instructions prior to being released from the hospital. In addition, private practices that provide Reiki treatment to all types of patients may also be helpful in helping new patients how to conduct basic Reiki self-care at home using a simple process of preparation and 10 different hand positions.

Preparation for self-treatment

Before beginning actual treatment, all practitioners interested in self-care should follow the following steps to ensure successful preparation:

1. Establish a regular schedule for self-

treatment. You should reserve time every day. Generally, patients can begin a 20-minute self-treatment session in the morning right after waking up, with a second 20-minute self-treatment session at the end of the day just before going to bed. These time limits are suggestions; if you feel comfortable or have more time available, you can extend these sessions to 30 or 60 minutes. Morning and evening are perhaps the best time for self-treatment, but you can adjust the time of day to fit your schedule.

2. Patients should perform Reiki self-treatment whether or not they feel well. Because Reiki self-treatment gives you an opportunity to set aside time during the day to counteract the effects of stress and worry, self-treatment is even more important when you are not feeling your best.

3. Find a safe, comfortable, and secluded space in your home. Ensure the space includes a chair in which you can sit comfortably or a bed or a sofa upon which you can lie down. This is where you will perform your self-treatment sessions. Do your best to use the same space regularly.

4. To begin preparation, sit quietly in meditation

in the quiet and secluded area you have chosen. It is best to perform self-treatment alone, but you can have someone present in the room if you need help for your care and safety.

5. Ensure you have created a quiet environment free of distractions and outside noise. Some patients find relaxing instrumental music during meditation and self-treatment, but if you find this to be a distraction, you can also conduct self-treatment in silence.

6. Remove your shoes. If you are lying on your back, place one pillow under your head and a second rolled-up pillow under your knees. You may use a blanket over your body to stay warm.

7. Close your eyes. Relax your body and mind. Before beginning treatment and as you enter a state of quiet meditation, reflect upon the nature of Reiki as the Universal Life Force that exists naturally within everyone. Remember that drawing upon Reiki energy strengthens the body's natural ability to heal itself.

8. Look and feel within as you notice and make a mental note of any places in your body or mind that need attention during your session. Remind yourself that your self-

treatment session is being performed only for the highest and greatest good.

9. Begin inhaling and exhaling using relaxed breaths, which you will maintain throughout your self-treatment session. If you find your attention drifting, focus once again on your breathing and body throughout the remainder of your session.

Self-treatment process

Again, it is important to remember that there is not exactly one way to conduct Reiki treatment sessions. Although specific cases may vary, the following overview of ten basic hand positions can help you formulate an initial understanding of how to conduct Reiki self-treatment. As soon as you complete the preparation activities, you may begin the self-treatment:

- First Hand Position:

Begin self-treatment by placing your hands together in prayer position. Your hands should occupy the middle region of your chest, just below your chin. With your eyes closed, focus on your inhalations and exhalations, breathing in and out fully, completely, slowly, and deeply to encourage complete relaxation of mind and body. Remain in this position for one to two minutes.

- Second Hand Position:

Place both hands on the top of the head at the location of the crown chakra. Continue your slow, steady inhalations and exhalations. Focus your attention on the touch of your hands to the top of your head, as the muscles and skin on your head all slowly relax. Maintain this position for one to two minutes.

- Third Hand Position:

Move both hands to cover your eyes, with your palms open and pressed gently against your face. Continue your steady breathing and shift your attention from your head to your eyes. Avoid covering your nose as you allow the touch of your hands to help relax the muscles and skin of your forehead, face, and eyes. Maintain this potion for two minutes.

- Fourth Hand Position:

Move your right hand down to gently cover your throat and left hand to gently cover your heart. Continue your deep, slow, steady inhalations and exhalations. Ensure that your right hand is not placed to firmly on your throat, so that you will not block the flow of air as you breathe.

Focus on your throat and your heart and relax the muscles in your neck, throat, and upper chest. Maintain this position for two minutes.

- Fifth Hand Position:

Move both hands together, with palms facing your body, to just below the breast line, with the tips of the middle fingers touching each other. Continue deep, steady inhalations and exhalations, as you focus on relaxing the muscles in the region of the lower chest. Maintain this position for two minutes.

- Sixth Hand Position:

Leaving your hands in the same position— facing inward with the tips of the middle fingers touching each other—move them together down to above the region of the upper stomach and solar plexus. As you continue slow, steady breathing, focus on your hands' proximity to this region enables the muscles of the abdomen to relax, Maintain this potion for two minutes.

- Seventh Hand Position:

Move the hands, again with the palms facing inward and the tips of the middle fingers touching, to the lower stomach region, just over the navel. Continue deep, steady inhalations and exhalations and allow the warmth of the energy conducted by your hands soften the muscles in this region and help them to relax. Maintain this position for two minutes.

- Eighth Hand Position:

Next, move both hands upward and gently place them on each of the shoulder muscles. As you continue your slow-deep, steady breathing, focus your attention to the upper extremities and the muscles in your shoulders and feel how the presence of your hands there helps release the tensions and allows the muscles to relax. Maintain this position for two minutes.

- Ninth Hand Position:

Now, move the hands to cover the area just above the waistline, at the lower back, where the kidneys are located. Continue deep, steady inhalations and exhalations, and focus on the transfer of energy to this area as the muscles relax and tension is released. Maintain this position for two minutes.

- Tenth Hand Position:

Finally, while in a seated or prone position, place each of your hands on each of your feet. If you find it easier, you can cross the left leg over the right knee and vice-versa. Focus on the healing energy transferred from your hands to the tops of your feet as you continue slow, steady breathing. Maintain this position for two minutes.

- Setting the Environment

Before providing Reiki treatment to any patients or students—or even to administer self-care—the Reiki practitioner must spend some time channeling Reiki to establish an environment that is conducive to healing and recovery. Chapter 2 discusses the Three Pillars of Reiki. The first of the three pillars-Gassho—is instrumental in effectively setting an environment appropriate to conducting Reiki healing sessions.

To initiate a session, Reiki practitioners must not only prepare themselves to ensure they have occupied a state of consciousness and receptivity that will allow them to impart healing energy, but also must prepare the room and the setting in which the treatment is to occur. Remember that Reiki healing works by enabling an attraction, distribution, and shift of energy; if the healing space in which a Reiki practitioner is working is constantly disrupted or bombarded by negative energy, the healing session will necessarily be less effective.

The first step in this process is for the practitioner to prepare the physical room or setting in which healing will take place. By setting the environment, practitioners can ensure optimum healing. Some practitioners may burn herbs like sage or light candles in colors associated with certain types of healing. Practitioners who use an intake form may review the ailments and illnesses for which their student or prospective patient is seeking treatment. If there are particular colors, smells, or herbs associated with healing in this area, they can be used to ensure healing for that particular patient is optimized.

Practitioners who have received the symbols from Second and Third Degree training should draw those symbols over themselves or in the air throughout the setting to create a safe and protected environment in which negative energy is repulsed.

Next, after successfully addressing the needs of the physical treatment setting, the practitioner's first priority should be their own spiritual preparation. As a surgeon must engage in a thorough process of physical hygiene prior to any operation to eliminate the risk of bacterial infection, so a Reiki practitioner must engage in a process of spiritual hygiene to eliminate the risk of disruption by the inclusion of negative energy. This step is accomplished by entering a state of gassho.

Sit quietly in the center of the room where treatment will occur. Place your hands, palms together, in prayer position. Begin breathing slowly and steadily, focusing on the energy entering your body as you inhale, and the energy leaving your body as you exhale. Focus thoughts of your physical body on the point where your middle fingertips tips meet.

With your consciousness focused only on your breathing and the touch of your middle fingers, you should feel obsessions with the demands of the outside world begin to slip away. As your mind clears and the tension is replaced with calm, the demands of your ego slip further away, and you will become open to contentment, peace, and happiness with your own existing state. At this point, you should begin to invite mindfulness, directing it toward the attraction of Reiki healing energy, with the goal of igniting this energy during treatment. The practitioner should remain in this state of gassho for at least 5 to 10 minutes.

Practitioners who have successfully prepared the physical environment to meet the needs of the patient and who have achieved a state of gassho may then invite the patient into the healing space.

Attunement

Reiki healing treatment sessions are distinct from attunement sessions. Though they are related, treatment sessions involve the movement of energy within a patient's aura by a practitioner who has previously been attuned. Thus, the patient in a treatment session receives treatment, but not attunement.

Reiki attunement itself is considered to be a fairly significant spiritual experience. Attunement is a necessary part of Reiki teaching and training and can only be performed by a Reiki Master. During the attunement process, the Reiki Master opens the chakras located in the student's crown, heart, and palms, and a special link is established to permanently connect the student to the Reiki source.

The source of Reiki is Rei, or God-consciousness. Through the Reiki Master, the student is attuned by receiving Reiki channeled directly from the source, through the hands of the

Reiki Master, and then into the student's aura through the newly opened pathways at the chakras. An attunement is a formal ceremony, and it may be attended by additional guides to ensure success. Manty students have indicated that attunement can bring about dramatic and profound mystical experiences, including deep healing, visions, past life visitation, and personal spiritual messages. Others have reported increased sensitivity and activity of the third-eye chakra, enhanced intuition, or an improvement in their ability to engage in psychic reading.

Once attunement takes place, the connection between the student and the Reiki source is permanent and lasts for the remainder of the student's life. Although it doesn't wear off, additional attunements, as well as daily practice, can increase the student's ability to access Reiki's healing energy, both in terms of volume and intensity. Generally, one attunement per level is all that is required, but as students receive additional attunements, they will be better able to achieve clarity of mind during gassho; heal their personal spiritual problems, as well as those of their clients and patients; and attain a higher level of consciousness and awareness.

As practitioners should prepare for treatment by completing a process of spiritual cleansing and clarification, so students should prepare themselves for attunement by ensuring they are as free of disruptions and toxicity as possible. The following steps have been suggested as helpful in preparing for attunement:

- For at least three days prior to attunement, maintain a strictly organic, vegetarian diet to ensure your system is free of pesticides, hormones, chemicals, or other artificial or harmful substances.

- Especially if you already eat a vegetarian diet, you may fast for one to three days prior to the attunement, drinking only water or juice. Be sure to consult with a dietician if you are inexperienced with fasting or have any special health needs.

- Avoid caffeine for at least three days prior to the attunement. Coffee, tea, and other caffeinated drinks can create imbalances in the nervous and endocrine systems, so make sure you do not drink any caffeinated beverages on the day of the attunement.

- Do not drink any alcoholic beverages for at least three days prior to the attunement.

- Avoid sugary foods like chocolate.

- If you have not quit already, try not to smoke for as long as possible prior to the attunement.

- During the week prior to the attunement, spend at least one hour per day in meditation. Focus on releasing tensions and negative emotions, such as anger, fear, jealousy, hate, and worry. Every day create sacred space within you and around you.

- To ensure your mind is an open and receptive blank slate, avoid watching television, listening to the radio, and reading newspapers. Instead, spend time going for quiet walks, exercising, and spending time in natural settings.

- Reiki is a discipline through which you will learn to impart healing. Although it is not itself a religion, you may find the conventions of your own religion to be helpful in preparing yourself to enter a higher state of spiritual consciousness.

Additional Concerns

Standards

To be successful as a Reiki practitioner, you must regard this undertaking as a lifelong commitment. Though unregulated by any external governmental regulatory authority, the global community of Reiki practitioners are self-regulating and have made a concerted effort to uphold and maintain standards throughout the field.

There are many professional associations for Reiki practitioners throughout the world, including the International Association of Reiki Professionals (IARP), the International Reiki Organization (IRO), the International House of Reiki (IHR), and The Reiki Alliance (RA). These organizations may offer many benefits to members, including information, education, and training; employment opportunities; continuing education; and more.

Fees

Costs of Reiki training may vary from one training school or institute to the next. Reiki was established as a professional practice in Japan, a culture that has a very different value system than many Western societies. Reiki practice depends upon the practitioner's freely chosen decision to engage in Reiki healing exclusively for the highest and most altruistic of purposes.

Many Reiki professionals willingly adhere

to this foundational principle. However, the absence of any accountable training system can present a challenge when verifying the authenticity and legitimacy of any given Reiki training program. When Dr. Tanaka introduced Reiki to Western audiences, she was aware of the conflict between fundamentally different value systems of Japan and the West. To bridge this gap, she required a fee of $10,000 for attunement. Her intention was to instill in the Western mind the appropriate level of respect for the professionalism and seriousness of Reiki by using money, which in the West has corresponded to the degree to which people accord respect and credibility to professional practice.

Many practices still use this $10,000 fee as the threshold fee for attunement, both to ensure the seriousness of the student's commitment and to communicate to students the seriousness with which they regard their own Reiki training program. However, many training institutes have begun adjusting this fee to enable a wider demographic—including those without access to this kind of funding—to become part of the community of Reiki healers.

Questions to consider

As you consider whether to make the commitment to becoming a professional Reiki healer, you should take some time to ask yourself some questions, and also to interview potential teachers. The following list is a suggestion that can help you get started laying a successful foundation for your career as a healer:

- Am I ready to make a serious commitment to studying Reiki?

- What does my heart and my instinct tell me about this area of practice?

- What does my heart and my instinct tell me about the schools and teachers I have considered?

- Can I set aside the time and energy to commit to a regular practice and study?

- What do the schools I am considering cover in their classes?

- How many hours of class time are required for certification?

- How much time training time is instructional versus hands-on practice?

- What is the school's relationship and view of

the lineage of Reiki teaching and practice?

- What does this school expect students to experience during attunement?

- What are the fees charged at this school?

- How long does the school recommend waiting between the various levels of training?

- Does the school offer any support?

- Are there any support groups in my area?

CHAPTER - 5
THE BENEFITS OF REIKI HEALING

The aim of Western medicine is to provide a definitive cure for a physical illness that has been officially diagnosed according to practices established by the scientific community. Obviously, Western medicine has tremendous value and is used every day to help people who have suffered injuries or contracted diseases to return to a state of physical well-being. Reiki is fundamentally different in that instead of relying on outside intervention to restore a state of physical well-being, it relies on the body's own intrinsic ability to heal itself. Thus, rather than introducing external interventions into the patient's system, the Reiki healer restores the patient's own healing powers to encourage long-term well-being.

As a result, the benefits of Reiki healing vary widely from the typical benefits associated with medical treatment. Many people have attested to Reiki healing's ability to cure acute physical ailments. However, the true benefits of Reiki lie in its ability to impart to both patient and practitioner a lasting state of health and vitality that not only aids in the recovery of past illnesses, but also encourages resistance to future illness and disease. In addition, Reiki healing moves beyond merely the physical and treats the whole patient, leading to improved self-care, spiritual growth, and a restoration of purpose and motivation.

Reduce Depression and Anxiety

Medical science has classified depression as a mood disorder accompanied by feelings of sadness, loss, regret, or anger to such a degree that they interfere with daily activities and a person's ability to function at a normal, productive level. Depression can interfere with activities such as daily work, leading to lost time and productivity; it can also cause damage to relationships, and in some cases can result in the development of chronic illnesses and other health conditions.

Patients suffering from depression also run the risk of exacerbating or further complicating other medical conditions, such as arthritis, asthma, cardiovascular disease, cancer, diabetes, and obesity. If these conditions worse, the depression can worsen, leading to a cycle of deteriorating health.

Simple feeling sad or angry alone does not mean you are depressed. However, if feelings of sadness, despair, listlessness, or hopelessness occur on a regular, ongoing basis, you may be suffering from depression. Symptoms of depression include irritable and negative moods, such as anger, aggression, and irritability; negative emotional states, such as sadness and emptiness; changes in behavior, such as a loss of interest in activities that used to bring pleasure; excessive drinking or drug use; sexual dysfunction; an inability to concentrate and focus; problems sleeping; and physical problems, such as fatigue, headaches, and digestive problems.

Anxiety is related to depression and is defined as a condition in which people have "recurring intrusive thoughts or concerns" (Felman, 2018). If anxiety worsens to the point that it becomes a medical diagnosis, it can interfere with a person's ability to function normally. Symptoms of anxiety include uncontrollable feelings of restlessness and excessive worry;

increased irritability; difficulty concentrating or focusing; and problems falling asleep or staying asleep. Anxiety may be diagnosed as general anxiety disorder (GAD), which is characterized by excessive, ongoing anxiety and worry about non-specific events, situations, or concerns. Some patients suffer from panic disorder, which manifests itself as brief and sudden but ongoing attacks of intense fear and terror, combined with shaking, confusion, and breathing difficulties. There are also many phobias specific to certain objects or experiences which may also be classified as anxiety disorders.

Western medicine commonly treats anxiety and depression with a combination of psychotherapy, medication, and behavioral therapy. Patients may take anti-depressant medication or other types of sedatives, and in cases in which these conditions result from trauma, psychotherapy can help patients identify the underlying issues causing their illness.

At some point, patients suffering from these illnesses are advised to seek alternative treatments to ensure long-term recovery. Medication and psychotherapy are effective, especially in the short-term, but often these treatments can become secondary addictions, and act as obstacles to making progress toward a more complete recovery.

Reiki can help patients recover from these illnesses by providing them with the tools to better manage self-care. By treating patients without medication and helping them redirect their bodies' naturally occurring self-healing properties, Reiki can help patients achieve a genuine and lasting recovery. In addition, Western medicine's approach lacks Reiki's capacity to open the door to further intellectual, spiritual, and personal growth and development. By providing patients with a foundation to grow outside the strict and often punitive confines of the environments that may have led to their disease, Reiki healing treatments may ultimately be the best hope for patients who suffer from these potentially grave and deadly illnesses.

Improve Medical Conditions

Reiki is often criticized as a valid form of medical treatment because it is so difficult to produce hard, statistical evidence proving its effectiveness in this area. However, researchers have begun to compile results from many case studies and clinical studies that the beneficial effects of Reiki can translate directly to the treatment of physical illnesses.

Relieve pain

Reiki works by drawing on the body's naturally occurring ability to heal itself. Often, this capacity for self-healing may be compromised for any of a number of reasons, some of which may be physical. For example, patients undergoing treatment for cancer, new mothers experiencing the pain of childbirth or Cesarean delivery, and patients undergoing treatment for back pain associated with herniated disks have all reported significant reductions in physical pain, pain-related stress and anxiety, and the need for analgesic painkillers. In addition, Reiki is a less expensive treatment alternative and had the added benefit of reducing blood pressure and pulse rates without the side effects of medication.

Many people discount Reiki because it appears to involve nothing more than a sequence of hand placements by the Reiki practitioner on various parts of the patient's body. The underlying foundation of Reiki healing is that these hand placements restore balance to the flow of energy, restoring and enhancing the body's natural capacity for self-healing.

Especially in the West, many people may be skeptical of these claims, so medical scientists have recently conducted tests to determine whether the claims of Reiki practitioners can be proven in a clinical setting. In 2000, researchers at the University of Colorado Medical School conducted an experiment to determine whether the treatment provided by trained Reiki practitioners was significantly different from the treatment provided by untrained people who merely mimicked their hand placements. They also wanted to determine whether Reiki treatment was only working as a suggestive, placebo effect.

Contemporary Western medicine currently uses electromagnetic treatment equipment to accelerate the healing of bone, skin, and other tissues and organs. Using this treatment model as the control, the researchers measured the vibrational frequencies coming from the hands and bodies of trained Reiki practitioners and people with no Reiki training or attunement. The study found that the trained Reiki professionals emitted electromagnetic vibrations in the range of 0.3Hz to 30Hz, with the most frequent reading occurring at 7 to 8Hz. These ranges were consistent with measurements testing whether living tissues and organs are healthy and were significantly different from the vibrations emitted by non-trained individuals. The study also employed Kirilian photography to provide a visual illustration of the energy emitted by the hands of trained Reiki practitioners (Moore, n.d.).

In another study at New York Presbyterian Hospital, a blind, random study compared the results of the effects of Reiki treatment on the autonomic nervous system. The study included three groups—a group treated by trained Reiki practitioners, a "sham" group treated by untrained personnel with no experience in Reiki, and a control group that received conventional treatment. The results indicated that patients who received Reiki treatments from trained practitioners showed reductions in pain and pain-related stress and anxiety, comparable with patients who were treated using conventional methods. These patients reported significantly more improvement than the patients in the "sham" group, who received only a placebo.

Pain is your body's way of communicating to you that something is wrong. Pain can result from a variety of sources— acute physical injuries, treatments for serious illnesses like cancer, post-operative recovery, childbirth, chronic conditions such as arthritis, and even psychosomatic pain resulting from psychological trauma. Medication is often the first response for treating pain, but medication is designed to treat pain as a symptom, rather than its underlying cause.

Although the body does have an amazing capacity for self-healing and recovery, this function can be compromised when we are physically ill or suffering from stress-related conditions. The pain is the normal indication of this dysfunction. As with long-distance runners who know that by the time they feel thirsty, they have waited too long to drink water and are already dehydrated, so people who experience pain may understand that they have waited too long to address the underlying illness that has compromised their capacity to self-heal.

Reiki can restore the natural, healthy vibration of electromagnetic energy within the aura and the physical body, so that tissues, organs and glands can redirect away from defending against trauma and back toward the maintenance of health. Once this balance is restored, the patient's reduced levels of anxiety and worry allow the healing process to accelerate. As a result, the causes of pain are more completely addressed, and pain as a symptom can be more effectively relieved.

Increase white blood cell production

The ability of your body to produce white blood cells has a direct effect on your body's immune system and your ability to fight off and recover from diseases and illnesses. Low white blood production may result from a variety of ailments, including viral infections, some disorders present at birth that affect the function of bone marrow, cancer, autoimmune disorders like HIV/AIDS, severe infections that require the use of large amounts of white blood cells, and some types of medications, such as antibiotics.

Often people may suffer from illnesses brought about specifically due to an insufficient production of white blood cells. Other times decreased white blood cell production may result from medical treatment itself. Either way, people who experience deficiencies in this area may have greater difficulty recovering from diseases and illnesses.

In another study, one group of patients was treated for this condition using Reiki. Another group was told simply to spend time relaxing. A third group was given no treatment recommendations at all. Tests before and after the trial period showed that subjects who had undergone Reiki treatment demonstrated an increase in white blood cell production; subjects in the other two groups showed no change.

By helping patients lower their stress and anxiety level, their immune systems are not taxed so heavily. As a result, their capacity for producing and storing white blood cells increases, and their level of healthfulness and resistance to infections like the common cold and other viruses can markedly improve.

Boost Intuition and Creativity

Of course, not everything that Reiki is used for involves illness, disease, and dysfunction. But even when we are healthy and feeling fine, there may be areas of our lives that remain on the fringes. When we get caught up in the business of our day-to-day routines, we may find contentment or even some degree of happiness, but often we may be left feeling that something is amiss. Though we can't seem to put our finger on the problem, this sense that something is missing can follow us around, and in some cases, even lead us back into a cycle of depression and anxiety. Reiki can help us build on an established foundation of personal success and health by helping us develop our capacity for intuition and creativity.

Intuition is the natural, instinctual response we may have toward people or situations. If you have ever been to a job interview, out on a date, or faced with the prospect of a new business venture, and felt in your gut that the job was wrong for you, that the person you were dating would be a bad influence in your life, or that the new business venture would end in financial damage, then you know what it is to listen to your intuition.

The intuition can be a difficult source of information to introduce into any decision-making process. Especially in the West, we respect the accuracy and verifiability of factual information and rational analysis. We have all seen what happens when financial managers and political leaders disregard the facts and make decisions based entirely on their gut— usually nothing good comes of it. At the same time, when you are faced with an important decision in business or in your personal life, and all the facts and rational analysis point to one answer, while your intuition points to another, you may find yourself at a crossroads and unable to make an informed decision.

What are the reasons for these conflicts? Often, political and business leaders choose to "go with their gut" because it's easier than rational analysis and trusting your intuition can have great appeal to the larger public. Similarly, corrupt elements in business and in personal relationships often take for granted the trusting and naïve nature of innocent people and may intentionally skew the facts in such a way as to tempt people to betray their intuition in the face of convincing factual evidence.

Either way, trusting your intuition takes no less of a commitment of time, energy, and seriousness as constructing a system of scientific analysis as a means of making decisions. No one would suggest that you should abandon a sober analysis of facts and evidence in your daily efforts to build success and happiness. But neither should you ignore your intuition. As when you spend time ensuring the validity and credibility of your information sources when analyzing options in a decision-making process, so you must ensure that your energy is clean, balanced, open, and free of impairments and blockages to ensure that your intuition will not mislead you.

Creativity is similar to intuition. Often, we find that we have reduced our lives to simply "going through the motions." We may have established a comfortable routine or grown accustomed to a particular way of doing things. Though the reliability and dependability of familiarity can be comforting and even necessary to help us feel secure and safe in our surroundings, we can sometimes fall into the trap of accomplishing less than we could or asking less of ourselves than is necessary.

When we get too comfortable, we can lose the creative drive and energy that prompted us to pursue the goal and the path in life we chose so long ago. This absence of creativity can lead to a washed-out and inspired feeling, and a sense of disillusionment or disappointment. Ignoring these signs can lead back into a state of boredom, which can in turn lead to depression and anxiety. Instead, regard these feelings as an indication that it is time to address some of the internal mechanisms of your psychological and spiritual outlook.

There are many steps you can take to keep your mind clear of corruptions and distractions. One common and widely used practice is keeping a journal. Journals provide a way for you to access your inner thoughts in a way that allows you to be honest with yourself and those around you with privacy, discretion, and without confrontation. Using a journal can help spark the flame of intuition by providing a blank canvas for honestly assessing what you believe the pros and cons of a given situation may be.

Similarly, deliberately taking a break from your work routine can help inspire your creativity. Whenever you have the opportunity, interrupt your routine and instead read a book, or watch a film, or spend time walking in natural surroundings. By "changing the channel," you give your subconscious an opportunity to reset itself and allow new energy to enter and revitalize you. You may discover that something you had not even considered may be the answer to the dilemma in which you find yourself.

Once you have successfully taken action to change direction by initiating new actions, you can turn to meditation and Reiki to further and deepen healing and recovery. Once your mind has been cleared of pre-conceptions and other mental obstacles, set aside time in a quiet and secluded area for meditation. If you have received First Degree Reiki Training, this would be an excellent opportunity for self-care.

Alternatively, if you are considering whether Reiki may help you "get unstuck," reviewing the reflections on your journal may be a great way to start a conversation with a Reiki practitioner.

Calm the Mind

Having a calm mind can be a difficult thing to achieve, especially in the chaotic, hectic, and demanding professional world. Often, we are conditioned to believe that the less at peace we are and the more stress we are willing to undertake, the greater will be our professional and financial reward. Working 60 to 100 hours per week, forgoing personal goals, and sacrificing everything for the success of the company does not necessarily lead to negative results. In fact, this very idea of selflessness lies at the center of much of the teachings in which Reiki is based.

However, your capacity for selflessness can be co-opted to serve interests that not only may not result in any direct benefit to you, but also may cause you considerable emotional, psychological, and spiritual harm. The good news is that there is no need for you to choose between one of the other. In fact, deep mediation using Reiki can help you achieve a calmness and serenity of the mind that can allow ultimately to dedicate more rather than less time to professional goals that once led to overwhelming stress and worry.

Reiki can help you reconnect the vibrant intelligence and rive your mind with your heart and with your higher self. By practicing self-treatment or scheduling cleansing and healing sessions with trained Reiki practitioner, you can reconnect with your center, absent the obstructive interference of your ego, and the petty concerns of materialism and vanity. By expelling these negative impulses that demand so much of your energy, all of your energy can be directed toward the pursuit of professional and personal goals, while simultaneously enabling your ability to act with confidence, decisiveness, and efficiency. Your mind calmed by the healing power of Reiki will function more like the eye of the hurricane—regardless of the chaos and bluster all around you, your calm and serene presence at the center will serve you well.

Enable Spiritual and Emotional Growth and Healing

Of course, it is also important to remember that Reiki is the direct result of a personal search for meaning and purpose. Many people who initially seek Reiki treatments themselves may not be particularly inclined to pursue goals associated with emotional or spiritual growth. Regardless, the benefits of Reiki extend beyond its ability to heal deficiencies and ailments of either the physical, psychological, or emotional kind.

Many people may be tempted to regard Reiki as a form of treatment whose usefulness is finite and limited. Once they have revered from their physical illness and have been restored to good health, or once they have been rejuvenated psychologically, many people may not consider that there is any reason to continue the practice of Reiki healing.

However, the goals of Reiki are to target the whole person, rather than just treating a symptom of a disease or illness. Many of the challenges we face on both our personal and professional lives can be overwhelming. Too often, we tend to ignore the importance of these challenges when they do not result in serious illnesses that require medical intervention. Recovering from an illness of any kind is always welcome news, but most medical treatments do not include any component for helping you address the many challenges and questions you may have after you have recovered your health.

You may have recently undergone some type of major life change—perhaps you lost a job, experienced the death of a loved one, recovered from a serious illness, or have somehow been confronted with a negative experience that has forced you to question some of your most basic assumptions about life and the world.

Finding guidance to answer these difficult questions can be challenging. Sometimes traditional forms of therapy can be helpful. Many people also find it helpful to join support groups where they can meet others who have encountered similar difficulties. These healthy responses can be instrumental in helping you to adapt and make changes.

Incorporating Reiki into this blend of behavioral, lifestyle, and even medical changes can often make the difference between success and failure. Though we rarely like to admit it, significant life changes may be better understood as the normal course of events rather than an unexpected turn. Especially if you are undergoing a period of grief, mourning, or loss, viewing these changes as an opportunity for growth may even sound cynical. Regular practice of Reiki can help clear internal blockages and obstructions so that your path to personal and spiritual growth and development can continue in a way that is healthy and rewarding.

Improve Self-Care Habits

The world has always been a money-conscious place, perhaps more so now than ever. Most of us have grown accustomed to the cynicism of insurance companies and healthcare providers who are usually reluctant to provide coverage or care to any but the least sick and the most affluent. Sadly, such policies usually create environments that only encourage more sickness, anxiety, and worry, and the cycle never seems to end.

Learning effective habits of self-care may be among the most important gifts you can give yourself. Regardless of your views about the rightness or wrongness of insurance companies who refuse to cover people who are not already healthy, these types of policies have a hand in determining the nature of the environments in which we all live and work.

Anyone can learn Reiki. First Degree Reiki training provides all students with an attunement and the basic skills to practice Reiki self-treatments, and that gift will last a lifetime.

At the same time, as awareness of problems within the medical and insurance industries grows, people are more interested in pursuing paths of self-reliance and self-determination as a means of counteracting the negativity of healthcare policies that are overly concerned with financial considerations. Skilled and trained Reiki practitioners are becoming more widely available everywhere in the world.

Whether you pursue Reiki healing as a patient or as a student, this restorative and powerful practice can help you establish a new path in life that leads to better overall physical and psychological health and fewer days spent missing work or quality time with your friends and family as a result of illness. As a system of self-care, Reiki also provides the unique benefit of helping you capitalize on your good health by giving you the tools to forge a new path, or re-energize your efforts as you continue to renew your dedication to pursuing value in your life and your relationships.

CHAPTER - 6

REIKI AND CHAKRAS

Reiki originates in Japanese spiritual and religious practice. The chakras originate in Hindu spiritual and religious practice. These two practices are vastly different in their approaches, yet they share many common core fundamental principles. Reiki literally means "universal life energy. Chakra literally means "wheel," and thus does not provide a direct link between the two systems. However, the chakras' purpose is to distribute a life energy known in Hindu tradition as "prana." Reiki is the equivalent of prana and provides a means of understanding the compatibility and complementary nature of these two systems of self-care.

This chapter discusses the specific details of how the chakras distribute prana through the energy body and how this system compares to Reiki healing practice. In addition, this chapter discusses how Reiki can stimulate and enhance the power of the chakras to create a lasting sense of health, vitality, and well-being.

The Seven Chakras

Western thoughts and medicine have become very heavily influenced by science and reason. Science and reason themselves are valuable and very important aspects of civilization and culture and achieving success and happiness without them would be extremely difficult. However, when we are faced with energy blockages and personal and spiritual challenges, the answers of Western psychology and psychiatry sometimes fall short. Although traditional psychotherapy may help you resolve many of the intellectual and emotional conflicts that exist in the psychological component of the brain, these solutions usually ignore that physical aspects of well-being that are necessary for you to attain the highest levels of functioning.

Reiki (Rei-Ki) is the practice of shifting energy. In Japanese, this energy is called Ki, in Chinese it is called Qi, and in Hindu it is called Prana. Reiki shares with the practice of Yoga the understanding that Ki, or Prana, is the key to long-term health and happiness. In Yoga, prana is distributed through chakras, or wheels of energy located throughout the energy body, or aura. As a result, an understanding of the chakras used in yoga is an essential component of learning how to successfully use Reiki as an energy healing technique. This section includes descriptions of each of the seven primary chakras used in most Western versions of yoga.

Before considering how Reiki can help you attain balance, health, vitality, and establish a foundation for success, take a few moments to try a brief experiment. Find somewhere comfortable, in a quiet, secluded area. Turn off the television, your mobile phone, the stereo, and any other devices. Site in a relaxed, natural position. You can sit on the floor, with your legs crossed, in yogi style, or anyway that feels natural and comfortable for you. Rest your hands gently on your knees or your lap. Close your eyes and begin breathing steady, full breaths, focus on the air entering your body as you inhale, then exiting your body as you exhale. Breathe through your nose. As you pay attention to your breathing with your eyes closed, feel your mind slowly relax and unwind, as all the preoccupations of the day recede and slowly fade away. Spend three to five minutes maintaining this state of quiet meditation.

When you are relaxed and calm, begin to visualize yourself walking along a natural path leading into a deeply wooded forest. Your feet are quiet on the soft, spongy earth, which is covered with grass and leaves, As you walk further into the forest, you feel yourself surrounded more and more by tall, towering trees. The sunlight is cool in the shade of the forest, and the light shines through only in speckled prisms and shafts through openings in the canopy of trees overhead. Birds are singing peacefully and happily all around you. You continue walking and the path takes a turn, Soon, the civilized world of highways and traffic lights and strip malls has completely disappeared from view, and you can hear nothing but the sounds of the forest. Up ahead, you hear the babbling of a small brook. The smell of the soil and trees is rich now and fills your nostrils with a clean, earthy scent. As you continue walking, you emerge into a heavily wooded clearing that dips down to touch the bank of the small river. You find a comfortable, soft spot covered with grass and moss and spongy earth and lie down next to the river. The sound of the water slowly rushing by, the birds chirping and singing overhead, and the wind slowly rustling through the trees fills you with peace and happiness.

When you have completed this meditation, slowly open your eyes as you come back to your surroundings. What did you feel? Warmth? Lightness? Happiness? Joy? Energy? Hope? Where did these feelings occur? In your arms? Your legs? Your chest and stomach? Your face, neck and throat? How would you describe the physical sensations associated with these feelings? Did you feel your energy flowing freely, easily, and without restrictions?

Now, try another exercise. Close your eyes again and begin breathing steady, full breaths, focus on the air entering your body as you inhale, then exiting your body as you exhale. Once more, breathe through your nose and focus on your breathing with your eyes closed, as you empty your mind of preoccupations and worry. Spend three to five minutes maintaining this state of quiet meditation.

When you are once again relaxed and calm, begin to visualize yourself at the office, or construction site, or retail store, or other place of business that you remember as your most unpleasant and unhappy time at work. Think about what happened on your unhappiest day at this employer. Remember the type of work you were doing, your colleagues, and your supervisor. Imagine yourself arriving at work after a hectic drive on the freeway. You are 30 minutes late, and you know will be lectured and possibly fired by your boss. You had an argument with a colleague the previous day, so you are reluctant to go into the office. Imagine yourself exiting your car, walking across the parking lot covered in asphalt, and approaching the front door. Focus on the feelings in your stomach area, your chest, your forehead behind your eyes, and your upper back.

When you have remembered this traumatic work experience, open your eyes and come back to your surroundings. What did you feel? Panic? Heaviness? Sadness? Depression? Anxiety? Anger? Despair? Where did these feelings occur? In your chest? Your arms and legs? Your back and forehead? How would you describe the physical sensations associated with these feelings? Was your energy blocked and constructed anywhere?

The exercises above can help you understand the crucial and important role energy plays in our ability to achieve happiness, success, and fulfillment. Even through this simple exercise, without leaving your room, you have proven to yourself that it is possible to shift the energy in your mind and body simply by focusing on one set of thoughts and beliefs over another.

The following descriptions will help you understand how energy is distributed through your body and where blockages may occur. Reiki healing results from a shift in energy to restore balance and flow and remove blockages, so an understanding of the basic anatomy of the energy body is essential.

1.   Root Chakra

The root chakra is located at the base of the spine in the area between the anus and the genitals. Energy from this chakra is associated with our most primal and basic necessities for survival, including food, shelter, and freedom from threats and danger. Energy at the root chakra is triggered by our "fight or flight" response. When we are denied basic life necessities, or when we are threatened with violence or theft or the violation of our personal space, we may instinctually function only from this very primitive and visceral center of energy, with our higher levels of consciousness blocked until stability can be restored.

If we can successfully meet the demands of the root chakra by securing for ourselves a safe home or dwelling, healthy food and water and a sense that we are free from any impending violations or challenges, the root chakra can also allow us to establish a positive connection with the earth that is often referred to as "grounding."

2.   Sacral Chakra

The sacral chakra is located in the region of the reproductive organs, in the lower abdomen, in front of the lower back. The sacral chakra is associated with the water element, our sexuality, and our ability to formulate intimate emotional bonds. Once we have established the safety demanded by the root chakra, we may feel protected enough to let our "inner child" or our "true self" emerge. Open, flowing, and balanced energy at the sacral chakra is necessary for us to feel comfortable and confident enough to risk being vulnerable in a close social environment.

The sacral chakra energy provides the means through which we can attain pleasure, depth of emotional expression, and sexual fulfillment. This is also the place from which we draw inspiration for creativity and self-expression. When energy from this region is blocked or impaired, me may experience emotional pain, guilt, and feelings of jealousy and inferiority.

3.   Solar Plexus Chakra

The solar plexus chakra is sometimes referred to as the "power chakra." It is located at the solar plexus, at the stomach level, in the region of the navel and is associated with the fire element. When the primitive and visceral energies of the root and sacral chakras have been satisfied, we are more able to enjoy the benefits of the transformative power of the solar plexus chakra. Whereas the first two chakras relate to personal, intimate needs and desires, the solar plexus chakra is where we draw energy to create and transform through our own efforts in the world.

Through this chakra, we gain feelings of confidence, self-esteem, and self-worth. A healthy solar plexus chakra can empower us to make decisions and take risks. Clearly, open and balanced energy at this level is necessary for so many of us in our professional lives. When this chakra is blocked or impaired, we may experience feelings of shame or embarrassment.

4.   Heart Chakra

The heart chakra is located at the center of the chest in the region before the heart. This chakra relates to our ability to feel and be motivated by love, compassion, and caring, not only for individual people, but also in a more general, selfless sense. The heart chakra also represents the bridge between the lower chakras that drive the needs of the physical self and the upper chakras that guide and empower the higher motivations of the spiritual self.

When the heart chakra is open and balanced, we can recognize what is of value in those things that have brought us satisfaction by acting with the energy of the lower chakras, allowing us to form relationships and make decisions motivated by unconditional love. However, when energy at this chakra is blocked, we may be overwhelmed by grief or motivated by selfishness.

5.   Throat Chakra

The throat chakra is the first of the three upper chakras and represents our ability to communicate the knowledge we gain through the wisdom of the heart chakra. Though we may be able to discover our true selves through meditation, prayer, and work at the level of the chakras, we are unable to activate and realize that knowledge to its full potential unless we can speak clearly and truthfully by drawing upon the energy of the throat chakra.

Through the throat chakra, we form a strong and important bond with our higher levels of consciousness. Without the ability to communicate these concerns, we may become frustrated in our efforts to fulfill what we have identified as our life's purpose. When energy at this chakra is blocked or impaired, we may resort to dishonesty or inaccuracy in our expression, which in turn can result in a lack of alignment throughout our energy system.

6.   Third Eye Chakra

The third eye chakra is located in the forehead, between the eyebrows, and above the nose. This chakra is called the third eye because through it, we can develop an inner vision and gain insight into our motivations and concerns at a more profound, deeper, and metaphysical level. This chakra represents the seat of intuition and knowledge, and it is a key component of making crucial decisions about the directions our lives should take and the formation of personal value systems, philosophies, and world views.

It is important to spend time reflecting on our existential motivations and goals, or we risk living in a state of metaphorical blindness, in which we allow ourselves simply to be pushed or pulled in whichever direction. Blockages and impairments at this level can lead to delusional thinking, misconceptions, and lack of clarity.

7.   Crown Chakra

Finally, the crown chakra is located at the region of the top of the head. As the root chakra connects us most directly to the most visceral and physical drives of our bodies, so the crown chakra connects us to the highest of all spiritual yearnings. This chakra connects us to pure consciousness itself, without regard to our own, personal life goals or concerns. Through the crown chakra, we are connected directly to the source of Reiki—Universal Life Energy itself.

When the crown chakra is properly activated, we can understand that we are in fact, not human beings on a spiritual journey, but spiritual beings on a human journey. We can engage with the divine power of existence at this level, and the energy that we draw in here can help to cleanse and energize our entire chakra system.

How Reiki Can Help Harness the Power of the Chakras

The tradition of chakra alignment and energy flow originates in ancient Hindu and tantric yoga practices. This spiritual belief system and its associated system of energy healing is distinct from other Eastern spiritual and medical traditions, including traditional Chinese medicine, as well as the traditions of Reiki healing established by Dr. Usui.

Although these practices are separate and distinct, they are also related and share many common traits. The previous section outlined the location of the chakras and their function in helping people attain spiritual energy balance by ensuring prana is distributed fluidly throughout the energy body. In the Japanese tradition, prana is called ki, and instead of chakras, practitioners refer to tandens.

Reiki practice is founded on a belief in one main energy center—the Seika tanden—which is located in the region before the lower abdomen, just below the navel. The location of this tanden corresponds roughly to the location of the sacral chakra in Hindu tradition. Altogether, there are three tandens in Japanese tradition—the Seika tanden, plus an additional tanden at the region of the upper chest, corresponding roughly to the heart chakra, and another at the forehead, corresponding roughly to the third-eye chakra.

Though these interpretations of energetic healing and spirituality differ in their specifics, they share a similar fundamental approach to holistic healing based in an understanding that complete health and vitality can only be achieved through a combination of physical, spiritual, and energetic healing. Open chakras enable your energetic body to receive the inflow of Reiki and makes possible the healing work of trained Reiki practitioners. Reiki, in fact, incorporates the chakra system directly into the training, attunement, and healing practices of Reiki teachers, healers, and patients.

All degrees of Reiki training require an attunement process. Regardless of the level, all Reiki practitioners undergo attunement. During this process, the Reiki Master opens the student's crown chakra and heart chakra. In addition, though not part of the traditional seven-chakra system most often used in Western practice, the Reiki Master will also open chakras located over the palms of the hands. With these four chakras opened and receptive to the inflow of Reiki, the new practitioner gains an increased ability to regulate and maintain the flow of healing electromagnetic energy through his or her own energetic body and to adjust and shift the flow of energy through the energetic systems of his or her patients.

Because the attunement process is permanent, all Reiki practitioners should make a conscious effort to continually maintain the health and openness of his or her chakras. When the chakras become blocked or impaired, the practitioner's ability to draw upon healing Reiki energy is diminished; this misalignment can be addressed by spending time in meditation to regain a clear and unblocked distribution of energy.

Perhaps more importantly, familiarity with the effect of energy flow through the chakras can help the practitioner detect, diagnose, and treat imbalances in the patient. By using a technique known as Byosen scanning, the skilled Reiki practitioner will look for impairments and blockages in the patient's aura. Often these disruptions will occur in the areas precisely where the chakras are located.

Obviously, when people suffer from traumatic physical injuries, such as broken bones, car accidents, physical assaults, or other types of accidents, diagnosing the cause of the associated pain is fairly easy. In addition, many physical illnesses and diseases resulting from bacterial or viral infections, or poor conditioning of vital organs often lead to physical discomfort. 139

However, many Reiki practitioners have reported that patients who complain of physical pain are often not suffering from any physical illness. The word "disease" is formed from the prefix, "dis," which means "not," and the base word "ease," which means free of difficulty. Thus, "diseases" are conditions in which patients are suffering from a state in which they are not free of impairment or difficulty. Quite frequently, Reiki practitioners have been able to detect that physical pain in the digestive tract, the neck, the back, and other areas of the physical body are not the result of any physical injury. Instead, there is often a blockage or impairment deep within the patient's energetic system. This absence of the free flow of energy results in a tendency to become physically tense, or to lose physical energy and muscle tone, ultimately leading to the emergence of physical symptoms of pain.

Because the physical body often reflects the health of our energy body, healing the energy body can help resolve the physical symptoms of illness and disease. In fact, many Reiki practitioners will use a generally agreed guide that helps them understand the ability of the seven-chakra system to influence health through the physical system of glands and organs. The glands and organs themselves are the physical means through which energy is distributed by the chakras. Each of the chakras, in turn, corresponds to one of the major glands, as follows:

- Root chakra: adrenal gland

- Sacral chakra: ovaries or testicles

- Solar plexus chakra: pancreas

- Heart chakra: thymus

- Throat chakra: thyroid gland

- Third eye chakra: pituitary gland

- Crown chakra: pineal gland

Modern medicine has shown us how the release of hormones and chemicals by these glands directly affects the ability of the body to grow, develop, heal, and react throughout our lives. Thus, when problems arise in the flow of energy through the chakras, physical constructions can impede the distribution of hormones and chemicals into the bloodstream, thereby resulting in the deterioration of our overall physical health.

The chakras can tell a skilled Reiki practitioner a great deal about what is going on in a patient's life. When the aura display signs of disruption, the location of the disruption may provide a clue about where and why the patient seems out of balance. In addition, whether each of the energy centers is overactive or underactive, open or blocked, often has a direct relation to many common life events, as follows:

- Root chakra: Blockages may result from traumatic events, major life changes, or serious conflicts in family relationships, often resulting in lower back pain, addictions, digestive problems like diarrhea and constipation, and pain in the groin, hips lower legs, and feet.

- Sacral chakra: Imbalances may occur as a result of sexual abuse or traumatic intimate relationships, resulting in deeply held feelings of anger and resentment, all of which can lead to pain in the lower back and pelvis, concerns about sexual adequacy, and negativity surrounding relationships, power, and control.

- Solar plexus chakra: Blockages here may occur whenever we have lost power or have suffered a blow to our self-esteem. Physically, these issues may manifest as eating disorders, liver dysfunction, ulcers, chronic fatigue, diabetes, or chronic indigestion.

- Heart chakra: Especially in the modern world, many of us experience intense loneliness and feelings of abandonment and alienation. This can lead to blockages in this chakra, which can manifest as congestive heart failure, asthma, lung or breast cancer, and bronchial pneumonia.

- Throat chakra: Blockages in this area can occur as a result of relationships in which we feel ourselves to be unfairly criticized or judged. Physical symptoms can include thyroid problems, chronic sore throat and coughing, swollen glands, and scoliosis.

- Third eye chakra: Any of the previous conditions can lead us to develop a lack of self-confidence and lose the ability to trust our own insights. When this happens, we may develop impairments at this chakra, which can result in brain problems like tumors, seizure disorders, and neurological disruptions.

- Crown chakra: The modern world presents new challenges to anyone trying to develop a coherent and lasting worldview grounded in healthy spirituality. The resulting alienation from the natural environment and our place in it can result in depression and chronic fatigue. Especially when there seems to be no corresponding physical illness or injury, healing of the energetic body can help resolve impairments.

Once again, Western culture and medicine are firmly based on empirical science and conventional medical intervention. Much of this tendency results in an increased ability to address acute and serious illnesses with a high degree of effectiveness, thoroughness, and efficiency. However, an overdependence on the ability of pills and surgeries to fix all of our problems in life can ironically make us sicker rather than healthier.

Using a more holistic approach, we can see that physical health is more the result of psychological, emotional, and spiritual well-being than the other way around. Furthermore, the physical work required to maintain psychological, emotional, and spiritual health often leads to increased levels of physical health and well-being.

Many Western doctors are trained to treat patients by examining the least invasive methods of treatment before resorting to more serious treatment options. By helping us gain awareness of the important function of the chakra system to our overall health and vitality, Reiki can be the most important weapon in the arsenal of preventive healthcare.

CONCLUSION

This book has provided a comprehensive overview of Reiki, a system of energy healing that can trace its modern forms back to Japan in the early 20th century. Although this lineage may account for many of the practices used by contemporary practitioners, the origins of Reiki can be traced back even further. Much of Reiki healing is based on beliefs that share common traits with other forms of Traditional Eastern medicine. "Ki," is the Japanese word for life energy, which in Chinese is known as "chi" or "qi," and in Hindu traditions as "prana." Despite the linguistic differences, each tradition regards with equal importance the distribution of life energy through an energy body that surrounds the physical body.

Reiki is unique among these other traditional forms of Eastern meditation and energy healing. Unlike yoga, tai chi, or other lesser-known mystical practices, Reiki has found its way into the mainstream of American medical and scientific communities. A minority of Reiki practitioners have asserted that Reiki is on par with many conventional forms of medical treatment in its ability to cure illnesses. Despite debates about this claim, emerging scientific studies and evidence have shown Reiki to be an invaluable component of conventional medical treatments, including treatments for serious illnesses like cancer. Reiki's widespread acceptance and use in hospitals throughout the United States and Europe, as well as its growing popularity around the world, prove its value as parts of a comprehensive system of self-care.

Reiki is also distinguished from other forms of alternative medicine in its established and formulated forms of training and certification. Although not officially regulated by any governmental regulatory authority, there are several international professional associations that allow Reiki practitioners to be very effective in self-regulating. The First Degree, Second Degree, and Third Degree levels of Reiki training provide a system of accountability and provide new practitioners and patients alike with a means of navigating and understanding the methods through which Reiki healing practices are administered.

By addressing the needs of the whole patient, Reiki provides a holistic system of health maintenance that works as well for healthy patients interested in self-growth and meditation as it does for people suffering from any of a wide range of psychological, emotional, and even physical illnesses. Patients and practitioners have attested to Reiki's ability to effectively treat depression and anxiety, relieve pain, boost immunity, vitality, endurance, and stamina, stimulate and inspire creativity and provide a foundation for exploring self-development and personal growth. Reiki's compatibility with the yogic traditions of the chakras, as well as its ability to complement many of the conventional practices of Western medicine, makes Reiki the perfect discipline for establishing a lifelong system of self-care.

Contemporary Western culture has successfully produced research, treatments, and medicine to treat, cure, and even eradicate countless illnesses and diseases that have plagued the world for centuries. Western science has enabled exploration of everything from space travel to digital computing to high-speed travel. These contributions have helped shape and transform human civilization and culture throughout history. Yet, the modern world has recently begun to lead us further from nature and deeper into a state of alienation from ourselves, from each other, and from the cultural traditions upon which our success and happiness depend. Modern conventional medical treatments have proven to be often miraculous in their ability to relieve suffering.

Yet, in the midst of these advances in science and technology, the benefits of the system of Reiki energy healing has become even more apparent. Our true nature as human beings and our need to address urgent spiritual, emotional, and psychological demands will not stop, no matter how far advanced we become in terms of technology and science. The simple and effective methods outlined in this book can help you restore the balance and harmony you need to attain a true and lasting sense of well-being and happiness.

RESOURCES

(n.d.). Retrieved from https://www.reiki-evolution.co.uk/the-history-of-reiki-healing/.

(n.d.). Retrieved from http://www.reikiworld.net/Reiki/Levels_of_Reiki.htm.

A Brief History of Reiki. (n.d.). Retrieved from https://reiki-light.co.uk/a-brief-history-of-reiki/.

A History of Reiki. (n.d.). Retrieved from https://www.thereikiguild.co.uk/topics/13-history-of-reiki.

A New Look at the Five Reiki Principles. (2018, January 25). Retrieved from https://iarp.org/new-look-five-reiki-principles/.

Admin. (2019, September 17). Reiki healing: What is Reiki? Retrieved from https://www.reikifed.co.uk/reiki-healing/.

Administrator, R. (2015, April 1). How does Reiki

work? Retrieved from https://www.reiki.org/faqs/how-does-reiki-work.

Administrator, R. (2015, April 2). Learning Reiki. Retrieved from https://www.reiki.org/faqs/learning-reiki.

Administrator, R. (2017, September 26). What is the history of Reiki? Retrieved from https://www.reiki.org/faqs/what-history-reiki.

Administrator, R. (2019, March 7). Usui/Tibetan Reiki class descriptions. Retrieved from https://www.reiki.org/usuitibetan-reiki-class-descriptions.

Alcantara, M. (2019, August 12). Your chakras are probably out of balance. Here's how Reiki can help. Retrieved from https://www.mindbodygreen.com/0-16807/your-chakras-are-probably-out-of-balance-heres-how-reiki-can-help.html.

Balance Five Elements with Reiki - Part 1 of 5 – Earth. (2015, December 10). Retrieved from https://reikirays.com/28285/balance-five-elements-with-reiki-part-1-of-5-earth/.

Balance Five Elements with Reiki - Part 2 of 5 – Water. (2016, January 5). Retrieved from https://reikirays.com/28325/balance-five-elements-with-reiki-part-2-of-5-water/.

Balance Five Elements with Reiki - Part 3 of 5 – Air. (2016, February 25). Retrieved from https://reikirays.com/29481/balance-five-elements-with-reiki-part-3-of-5-air/.

Balance Five Elements with Reiki - Part 4 of 5 – Fire. (2016, February 4). Retrieved from https://reikirays.com/29968/balance-five-elements-with-reiki-part-4-of-5-fire/.

 Can I Learn Reiki Myself? (n.d.). Retrieved from https://www.takingcharge.csh.umn.edu/can-i-learn-reiki-myself.

Can Reiki Help Speed Healing After Surgery? (2019, February 10). Retrieved from https://iarp.org/can-reiki-help-speed-healing-after-surgery/.

Chakra-Anatomy.com. (n.d.). Reiki principles. Retrieved from https://www.chakra-anatomy.com/reiki-principles.html.

Chakra-Anatomy.com. (n.d.). Benefits of Reiki. Retrieved from https://www.chakra-anatomy.com/benefits-of-reiki.html.

Crosthwaite, A. M. (2019, March 14). If you're interested in learning Reiki, read this first. Retrieved from https://www.mindbodygreen.

com/articles/what-is-reiki-and-how-does-it-work.

Dai Ko Myo Explained. (2015, December 16). Retrieved from https://reikirays.com/15113/dai-ko-myo-explained/.

Definitions for Gassho. (n.d.). Retrieved from https://www.definitions.net/definition/gassho.

The Three Degrees of Reiki. (n.d.). Retrieved from https://reiki-light.co.uk/the-three-degrees-of-reiki/.

Engaging in the Flow of Reiki through Its Three Pillars. (n.d.). Retrieved from https://www.authorkarenfrazier.com/blog/engaging-in-the-flow-of-reiki-through-its-three-pillars#/.

Felman, A. (2018, October 26). Anxiety: Overview, symptoms, causes, and treatments. Retrieved from https://www.medicalnewstoday.com/articles/323454.php#symptoms.

The Five Reiki Principles Taught by Dr. Usui. (n.d.). Retrieved from http://reikipathway.com/id42.html.

Five Reiki Principles. (n.d.). Retrieved from https://www.reiki-for-holistic-health.com/five-reiki-principles.html.

Fletcher, E., Walsch, N. D., Nichols, L., & Diamond, M. (2019, October 30). How to improve yourself with the 5 Reiki principles. Retrieved from https://blog.mindvalley.com/reiki-principles/.

Gassho. (n.d.). Retrieved from https://en.wiktionary.org/wiki/gassho.

History of Reiki. (2019, February 10). Retrieved from https://iarp.org/history-of-reiki/.

The History of Reiki - An Ancient Technique for Modern Life. (n.d.). Retrieved from https://www.thethirstysoul.com/reiki/history-of-reiki/.

Holland, V. H. and K. (2019, September 18). Depression: Symptoms, causes, treatment, and more. Retrieved from https://www.healthline.com/health/depression#symptoms.

Hosak, M., & Hosak, M. (2019, August 21). The five pillars of Reiki. Retrieved from http://www.shingon-reiki.com/the-five-pillars-of-reiki/.

How Does Reiki Work? (2019, February 12). Retrieved from https://iarp.org/how-does-reiki-work/.

How to Use Reiki to Balance the Chakras. (n.d.). Reiki & Chakra magazine. Retrieved from https://www.chakras.info/reiki/.

Hurst, K., & Hurst, K. (2019, June 3). What is Reiki? 7 Health benefits of Reiki treatments. Retrieved from http://www.thelawofattraction.com/7-benefits-reiki/.

Janet, Pauline, & Niamh. (n.d.). 11 benefits of Reiki treatments - Promotes harmony, balance, and peace. Retrieved from https://www.thethirstysoul.com/reiki/benefits-of-reiki/.

The Levels of Reiki Attunements. (n.d.). Retrieved from https://jerrymikutis.com/the-levels-of-reiki-attunements/.

Low White Blood Cell Count Causes. (2018, November 30). Retrieved from https://www.mayoclinic.org/symptoms/low-white-blood-cell-count/basics/causes/sym-20050615.

Newman, T. (2017, September 6). Reiki: What is it and are there benefits? Retrieved from https://www.medicalnewstoday.com/articles/308772.php.

Reading the Body's Energy and the Three Pillars of Reiki . (2017, April 10). Retrieved from https://reikirays.com/36894/reading-bodys-energy-three-pillars-reiki/.

Patel, K. (2019, June 19). Reiki healing for beginners. Retrieved from https://goop.com/

wellness/spirituality/reiki-for-beginners/.

Paul, N. L. (n.d.). Reiki for dummies cheat sheet. Retrieved from https://www.dummies.com/ health/reiki-for-dummies-cheat-sheet/.

Paul, N. L. (n.d.). The three levels of Reiki training. Retrieved from https://www.dummies.com/ health/the-three-levels-of-reiki-training/.

Pichereau, C. (n.d.). How Reiki works with the chakra system. Retrieved from https://www. dummies.com/religion/spirituality/how-reiki-works-with-the-chakra-system/.

Rebolini, A. (2017, September 25). What the heck happened to my body during Reiki? Retrieved from https://www.thecut.com/2017/09/what-the-heck-happened-to-my-body-during-reiki. html.

Reiki. (2019, November 14). Retrieved from https://en.wikipedia.org/wiki/Reiki.

Reiki & The Chakras - Bring the Body into Balance & Harmony. (n.d.). Retrieved from https://www. thethirstysoul.com/reiki/chakras-reiki/.

Reiki - A Basic Overview. (n.d.). Retrieved from https://www.wholepersonhealth.com/services/ reiki/.

Reiki and the Chakras: A Gateway for Opening Spiritual Gifts. (2016, December 22). Retrieved from https://iarp.org/reiki-and-the-chakras-gateway-for-opening-spiritual-gifts/.

Reiki and the Main Chakras. (n.d.). Relativt! Retrieved from http://www.reiki.nu/treatment/chakra/chakra.html.

Reiki English Info. (n.d.). Retrieved from https://usui-reiki-gakkai-polska.blogspot.com/p/english-info.html.

Reiki of 7 Levels Courses. (n.d.). Retrieved from https://www.naturesintentionsnaturopathy.com/reiki/reiki-7-levels.htm.

Reiki Levels of Attunement 1, 2 & 3 Explained. (2017, February 22). Retrieved from https://reikiguide.org/reiki-levels/.

Reiki Self-Treatment. (n.d.). Retrieved from https://my.clevelandclinic.org/health/treatments/21080-reiki-self-treatment.

Ronquillo, H. (2019, November 1). 5 Reiki principles to promote a healthy, loving life. Retrieved from https://www.mindbodygreen.com/0-15751/5-reiki-principles-to-promote-a-healthy-loving-life.html.

Ruhl, B. (2016, August 18). Reiki or theta

healing - Which energy healing process works better? Retrieved from https://medium.com/@barbruhl/reiki-or-theta-healing-which-energy-healing-process-works-better-e35087667d8c.

Schmidt, H. (2015, September 2). The five Reiki principles. Retrieved from http://www.zenshiwellness.com/blog/2016/1/5/the-five-reiki-principles.

The Six Principles of Reiki. (n.d.). Retrieved from https://www.healyourlife.com/the-six-principles-of-reiki.

The Three Pillars of Reiki. (2018, November 10). Retrieved from https://naturespathways.com/south-central-wisconsin-edition/september-2014-south-central-wisconsin-edition/the-three-pillars-of-reiki/.

Usui Shiki Ryoho - The Usui System of Reiki Healing. (n.d.). Retrieved from https://www.reikiassociation.net/usui-shiki-ryoho.php.

Vidal, M. (n.d.). The five elements. Retrieved from https://www.reikiactivo.com/en/other-things/taichi/the-five-elements.

What Is Reiki? (2019, February 12). Retrieved from https://iarp.org/what-is-reiki/.

Why Dr. Oz Has Embraced the Healing Powers

of Reiki. (2019, February 10). Retrieved from https://iarp.org/dr-oz-and-the-healing-power-of-reiki/.

The Wood Element. (n.d.). Retrieved from https://www.elementaltransformation.com/the-wood-element.html

CPSIA information can be obtained
at www.ICGtesting.com
Printed in the USA
LVHW080534261020
669798LV00006B/217